PIEDMONT TRAVEL GUIDE 2024

Your Essential Guide to Italy's Hidden Gem, Featuring Culinary Delights, Scenic Landscapes, and Local Secrets for the Ultimate Travel Experience in 2024

David C. Anaya

Copyright © 2024 [David C. Anaya]

All rights reserved. No part of this publication may be reproduced, distributed, or transmitted in any form or by any means, including photocopying, recording, or other electronic or mechanical methods, without the prior written permission of the publisher, except in the case of brief quotations embodied in critical reviews and certain other noncommercial uses permitted by copyright law.

TABLE OF CONTENTS

INTRODUCTION.................4
Chapter 1: Introduction to Piedmont....7
    A. Overview of the Region.................7
    B. Geography and Climate................ 10
    C. Cultural Significance............. 13
    D. 15 Lesser Known Facts about Piedmont. 17

Chapter 2: Getting to Piedmont...........23
    A. Transportation Options................ 23
    B. International Access Points..................29
    C. Local Transportation Within Piedmont.. 33

Chapter 3: Top Destinations in Piedmont..................... 38
    A. Turin (Torino)............... 38
    B. Alba.................42
    C. Asti................ 45
    D. Lake Maggiore................ 48
    E. Langhe Wine Region............ 52
    F. Barolo Wine Region................55

Chapter 4: Activities and Attractions.... 60
    A. Outdoor Activities...................60
    B. Historical Landmarks and Museums... 64
    C. Culinary Experiences..........68

Chapter 5: Accommodation Options...74
    A. Hotels..................74
    B. Bed and Breakfasts...............78
    C. Agriturismo (Farm Stays)..............82

Chapter 6: Dining and Cuisine............ 87
    A. Traditional Piedmontese Dishes.......... 87
    B. Recommended Restaurants and Eateries. 92
    C. Food Markets and Specialty Shops....... 96

Chapter 7: Practical Information.......101
    A. Language and Communication......... 101
    B. Currency and Money Matters
    C. Packing Lists for Piedmont
    D. Safety Tips and Emergency Contacts

Chapter 8: Piedmont for Families......110
    A. Family-friendly Attractions and Activities................. 110

B. Parks and Playgrounds........................ 114

   C. Kid-friendly Restaurants and
   Accommodations..................................... 117

Chapter 9: Itinerary Planning............122

   A. Sample Itineraries for 1 Week, 10 Days,
   and 2 Weeks...122

   B. Ten Days Itinerary................................124

   B. Day-by-Day Breakdown of Activities and
   Sightseeing... 127

   C. Tips for Maximizing Time and
   Experiences.. 131

**Chapter 10: Relaxation and Wellness
Retreats..135**

   A. Thermal Baths and Hot Springs......... 135

   B. Yoga and Meditation Retreats............ 137

CONCLUSION.. 141

INTRODUCTION

In the heart of a bustling city, amidst the daily hum of life, Mr. Christopher found himself yearning for something different, something beyond the ordinary. So, with a spark of spontaneity and a thirst for adventure, he embarked on a journey to Piedmont, Italy, in the spring of 2024.

As he stepped off the train in Turin, the crisp mountain air greeted him, infused with the scent of blooming flowers and anticipation. With his copy of the Piedmont travel guide in hand, Mr. Christopher set out to explore this enchanting region.

His first stop was Turin, the vibrant capital of Piedmont. Narrow streets led him to grand piazzas adorned with elegant fountains and historic cafes. With each step, he immersed himself in the city's rich history, marveling at the grandeur of the Royal Palace and the beauty of the Mole Antonelliana.

Guided by the book's recommendations, Mr. Christopher indulged in the culinary delights of Piedmont, savoring each bite of creamy risotto and decadent chocolate gianduja. He wandered through bustling food markets, sampling local cheeses and freshly picked truffles, each flavor igniting his senses and leaving him craving more.

But it was the Piedmontese countryside that truly captured Mr. Christopher's heart. Venturing into the rolling hills of Langhe, he discovered a landscape straight out of a painting—vast vineyards stretching as far as the eye could see, punctuated by ancient castles and picturesque villages clinging to the hillsides.

In the town of Alba, Mr. Christopher found himself swept up in the magic of the annual truffle festival. The air buzzed with excitement as locals and visitors alike gathered to celebrate this culinary treasure. With the help of the travel guide, he navigated the bustling streets, indulging in truffle-infused delicacies and joining in the lively festivities.

As the sun dipped below the horizon, Mr. Christopher found himself atop a hill overlooking the Piedmontese countryside, the glow of the setting sun casting a golden hue over the landscape. In that moment, surrounded by the beauty of Piedmont, he felt a sense of peace and contentment wash over him—a feeling he knew he would carry with him long after his journey had ended.

Reflecting on his unforgettable experience, Mr. Christopher realized the true value of his Piedmont travel guide. It had been more than just a book—it had been his companion, guiding him through the winding streets of Turin, introducing him to the flavors of Piedmont, and leading him to moments of pure magic. And as he boarded the train back home, he knew that Piedmont would always hold a special place in his heart—a place where dreams were born and memories were made.

PIEDMONT MAP

Chapter 1: Introduction to Piedmont

Piedmont, nestled in the northwest corner of Italy, captivates visitors with its unique blend of picturesque landscapes, rich history, and culinary delights. This enchanting region, often referred to as Piemonte in Italian, translates to "foot of the mountain," reflecting its stunning alpine scenery and rolling hills. As a seasoned traveler with two decades of exploration under my belt, I am excited to introduce you to the wonders of Piedmont through this comprehensive travel guide.

A. Overview of the Region

Piedmont, often referred to as "Piemonte" in Italian, is a region of remarkable diversity and cultural significance, situated in the northwest of Italy. Spanning an area of over 25,000 square kilometers, Piedmont is bordered by the majestic Alps to the north and the rolling hills of the Langhe and Monferrato regions to the south. This geographical diversity contributes to the region's rich tapestry of experiences, drawing travelers from far and wide to explore its treasures.

At the heart of Piedmont lies its bustling capital city, Turin. Steeped in history and culture, Turin serves as the perfect starting point for any journey through the region. Visitors are greeted by the city's elegant architecture, from the grandeur of Piazza Castello to the iconic Mole Antonelliana, which dominates the skyline. Turin is also renowned for its world-class museums, including the Egyptian Museum and the National Museum of Cinema, which showcase the region's rich cultural heritage.

Beyond the capital, Piedmont is a land of enchanting landscapes and charming towns waiting to be discovered. To the north, the towering peaks of the Alps provide a playground for outdoor enthusiasts, offering opportunities for skiing, snowboarding, and hiking amidst breathtaking scenery. The picturesque towns of Cuneo and Saluzzo offer glimpses into Piedmont's medieval past, with their well-preserved historic centers and imposing fortresses.

In the southern part of the region, the landscape transforms into a patchwork of vineyards, orchards, and rolling hills. The Langhe and Monferrato regions, both UNESCO World Heritage Sites, are renowned for their picturesque landscapes and world-class wines. Visitors can explore charming hilltop towns like Alba and Asti, sample the region's famous Barolo and Barbaresco wines, and indulge in the local culinary delights.

Piedmont's cultural significance extends beyond its architecture and landscapes to its vibrant culinary scene. The region is a food lover's paradise, boasting a rich gastronomic heritage influenced by its rural traditions and proximity to France and Switzerland. From hearty dishes like bagna cauda (a warm garlic and anchovy dip) and brasato al Barolo (beef braised in Barolo wine) to delicate pastries like gianduiotti (chocolate hazelnut treats), Piedmontese cuisine delights the senses and leaves a lasting impression on visitors.

Moreover, Piedmont is a region steeped in tradition and folklore, with colorful festivals and celebrations held throughout the year. From the historic Battle of the Oranges in Ivrea to the vibrant Palio di Asti horse race, these events offer a unique glimpse into Piedmont's cultural identity and provide unforgettable experiences for visitors.

In conclusion, Piedmont is a region of unparalleled beauty, rich history, and gastronomic delights waiting to be explored. Whether you're drawn to its majestic mountains, charming towns, or world-class cuisine, Piedmont offers something for everyone and promises to leave a lasting impression on all who visit.

B. Geography and Climate

Piedmont's geography and climate play integral roles in shaping the region's diverse landscapes, agricultural practices, and overall appeal to visitors. Situated in the northwest corner of Italy, Piedmont is bordered by the Alps to the north, the Apennine

Mountains to the west, and the Po River to the south and east. This strategic location at the foot of the mountains gives the region its name, "Piedmont," which translates to "foot of the mountain."

The Alps, with their snow-capped peaks and rugged terrain, dominate the northern part of Piedmont, offering a stunning backdrop for outdoor adventures year-round. Ski resorts like Sestriere and Bardonecchia attract winter sports enthusiasts from around the world, while the summer months beckon hikers, climbers, and nature lovers to explore the region's network of trails and alpine meadows.

In contrast to the mountainous north, the southern part of Piedmont is characterized by rolling hills, fertile plains, and picturesque vineyards. The Langhe and Monferrato regions, in particular, are renowned for their scenic landscapes and world-class wines, including Barolo, Barbaresco, and Moscato d'Asti. Visitors to this area can enjoy leisurely drives along winding country roads, stopping to sample wines at family-run vineyards and indulge in the region's rich culinary traditions.

Piedmont's geography also contributes to its diverse microclimates, with weather patterns varying significantly from one area to another. The region experiences a continental climate, with hot summers and cold winters, but local factors such as elevation, proximity to water sources, and exposure to prevailing winds can influence temperatures and precipitation levels. For example, the Po Valley, which stretches across the eastern part of Piedmont, tends to be warmer and drier than the mountainous areas to the north and west.

Throughout the region, agriculture plays a vital role in the local economy, with Piedmont's fertile soils and favorable climate supporting a wide range of crops and agricultural activities. In addition to vineyards, Piedmont is known for its production of hazelnuts, rice, and fruits such as peaches and cherries. The region's culinary traditions are deeply rooted in its agricultural heritage, with locally sourced ingredients featuring prominently in traditional dishes like risotto, agnolotti pasta, and tajarin.

Despite its diverse geography and microclimates, Piedmont is united by its breathtaking natural beauty, rich cultural heritage, and warm hospitality. Whether you're exploring the rugged peaks of the Alps, savoring the flavors of the Langhe wine country, or soaking in the vibrant atmosphere of Turin's bustling streets, Piedmont offers a wealth of experiences for travelers seeking adventure, relaxation, and immersion in Italian culture.

C. Cultural Significance

Piedmont's cultural significance is deeply rooted in its long and storied history, which spans centuries of political intrigue, artistic innovation, and culinary excellence. From its royal palaces and historic landmarks to its vibrant festivals and traditional cuisine, Piedmont offers a rich tapestry of experiences that celebrate the region's unique heritage.

One of the most enduring legacies of Piedmont's past is its association with the House of Savoy, a powerful dynasty that ruled over the region for centuries. The Savoyards left an indelible mark on Piedmont's landscape, commissioning grand palaces, ornate churches, and elegant gardens that still stand as testaments to their wealth and influence. The Royal Palace of Turin, the Palazzo Madama, and the Reggia di Venaria are just a few examples of the lavish residences built by the Savoyards, which now serve as museums and cultural landmarks.

Piedmont's capital city, Turin, is a treasure trove of cultural riches, boasting world-class museums, galleries, and architectural marvels. The Egyptian Museum, housed in a striking neoclassical building, is home to one of the most extensive collections of Egyptian artifacts outside of Cairo. The National Museum of Cinema, located in the iconic Mole Antonelliana, offers visitors a journey through the history of film, while the GAM (Gallery of Modern Art) showcases works by renowned Italian artists from the 19th and 20th centuries.

In addition to its architectural and artistic heritage, Piedmont is renowned for its culinary traditions, which reflect the region's rural roots and aristocratic influences. Piedmontese cuisine is characterized by its emphasis on fresh, locally sourced ingredients and simple yet flavorful preparations. Dishes like vitello tonnato (veal with tuna sauce), agnolotti del plin (filled pasta parcels), and bagna cauda (a warm dip made with garlic and anchovies) are beloved staples of Piedmontese cuisine, enjoyed by locals and visitors alike.

Piedmont is also famous for its wines, which rank among the finest in Italy and the world. The Langhe and Monferrato wine regions, with their terraced vineyards and picturesque landscapes, produce renowned varietals such as Barolo, Barbaresco, and Barbera. Wine lovers flock to Piedmont to sample these prized vintages and explore the historic wineries and cellars where they are produced.

Beyond its culinary and artistic heritage, Piedmont is a region steeped in tradition and folklore, with a calendar of festivals and celebrations that reflect its cultural diversity and community spirit. From the historic Palio di Asti horse race to the colorful Battle of the Oranges in Ivrea, these events offer visitors a glimpse into Piedmont's vibrant past and enduring traditions.

In conclusion, Piedmont's cultural significance lies in its rich history, artistic heritage, and culinary traditions, which come together to create a unique and unforgettable experience for visitors. Whether exploring the historic streets of Turin, savoring the flavors of Piedmontese cuisine, or participating in a traditional festival, travelers are sure to be captivated by the region's cultural richness and timeless charm.

D. 15 Lesser Known Facts about Piedmont

While Piedmont may be renowned for its iconic landmarks and world-class cuisine, the region is also home to a wealth of hidden gems and lesser-known treasures waiting to be discovered. From historic landmarks to culinary delights, here are 15 fascinating facts about Piedmont that will inspire you to explore this captivating corner of Italy:

1. University of Turin: Founded in 1404, the University of Turin is one of the oldest universities in Europe and the world, making it a prestigious center of learning and research.

2. Fiat Automobiles: Turin is the birthplace of Fiat Automobiles, one of Italy's most iconic car manufacturers. Founded in 1899 by Giovanni Agnelli, Fiat has played a significant role in shaping the automotive industry.

3. Shroud of Turin: The Cathedral of Saint John the Baptist in Turin houses the Shroud of Turin, a linen cloth believed by some to be the burial shroud of Jesus Christ. The shroud remains a subject of fascination and debate among scholars and believers.

4. Sacri Monti: Piedmont is home to the Sacri Monti (Sacred Mountains), a series of nine religious complexes featuring chapels, shrines, and sculptures dedicated to the life of Jesus Christ and the Virgin Mary. These UNESCO World Heritage Sites are cherished for their artistic and spiritual significance.

5. Langhe-Roero and Monferrato Vineyards: Designated UNESCO World Heritage Sites in 2014, the Langhe-Roero and Monferrato vineyard landscapes are celebrated for their outstanding cultural and natural value, as well as their contribution to winemaking traditions.

6. Palio di Asti: The Palio di Asti is one of Italy's oldest and most famous horse races, dating back to the 13th century. Held annually in the city of Asti, the Palio attracts thousands of spectators who gather to witness the thrilling spectacle.

7. Battle of the Oranges: Ivrea is known for its historic Battle of the Oranges, a unique carnival celebration that reenacts a medieval revolt against tyrannical rule. Participants engage in a spirited orange-throwing battle, commemorating the city's rebellious spirit.

8. Porta Palazzo Market: Turin is home to Europe's largest open-air market, the Porta Palazzo Market. Spanning over 50,000 square meters, the market offers a vibrant array of fresh produce, clothing, and artisanal goods, making it a must-visit destination for shoppers and food enthusiasts.

9. Alba Truffle Festival: Each autumn, the town of Alba hosts an annual truffle festival, celebrating the prized white truffles that grow abundantly in the region. The festival attracts truffle lovers from around the world who come to indulge in this luxurious culinary delicacy.

10. *Piedmontese Cuisine:* Piedmontese cuisine is renowned for its rich and hearty flavors, with dishes like tajarin pasta, bollito misto (mixed boiled meats), and carne cruda (raw meat tartare) showcasing the region's culinary heritage.

11. *Turin's Egyptian Museum:* The Egyptian Museum in Turin boasts the second-largest collection of Egyptian artifacts in the world, after the Cairo Museum. Visitors can explore over 30,000 artifacts spanning millennia of Egyptian history and culture.

12. *Royal Palace of Venaria:* Situated just outside Turin, the Royal Palace of Venaria is one of the largest royal residences in the world, surpassing even the Palace of Versailles in size. This magnificent Baroque palace and its sprawling gardens are a UNESCO World Heritage Site.

13. Gran Paradiso National Park: Piedmont is home to Italy's first national park, the Gran Paradiso National Park, established in 1922. Spanning over 70,000 hectares, the park is a haven for wildlife enthusiasts, offering opportunities to spot ibex, chamois, and other Alpine species.

14. Piedmontese Chocolate: Piedmont is renowned for its rich tradition of chocolate making, with iconic brands like Caffarel and Venchi originating in the region. Visitors can indulge in a variety of decadent chocolates and pralines, making for a sweet souvenir of their Piedmontese adventure.

15. Baroque Architecture: Piedmont's cities and towns are adorned with elegant Baroque architecture, with notable examples including the Basilica of Superga overlooking Turin and the Church of San Lorenzo in Turin's historic center. These stunning landmarks showcase the region's artistic and architectural heritage.

In conclusion, Piedmont's lesser-known facts reveal a region brimming with history, culture, and culinary delights waiting to be explored. Whether marveling at historic landmarks, indulging in local delicacies, or experiencing vibrant festivals, Piedmont offers a wealth of experiences for travelers seeking authentic Italian charm and hidden gems off the beaten path.

As you embark on your journey through Piedmont, allow yourself to be enchanted by its beauty, history, and flavors, and prepare to create memories that will last a lifetime.

Chapter 2: Getting to Piedmont

Piedmont, nestled in the northwest corner of Italy, is a region steeped in rich history, stunning landscapes, and culinary delights. Before you immerse yourself in its wonders, it's essential to know how to get there and navigate within the region efficiently.

A. Transportation Options

When planning your journey to Piedmont, it's essential to consider the various transportation options available to you. Each mode of transport offers its own unique benefits and can cater to different preferences and travel styles. Here's a closer look at the transportation options for reaching Piedmont:

1. Air:

Flying into one of Piedmont's main airports is often the most convenient option for international travelers. Turin-Caselle Airport (TRN), located approximately 16 kilometers northwest of Turin's city center, serves as the primary gateway to the region. From Turin-Caselle Airport, travelers can easily access popular destinations within Piedmont, such as the charming towns of Alba and Asti or the ski resorts of the Alps.

Example: If you're traveling from London to Piedmont. You can book a direct flight from London Heathrow Airport (LHR) to Turin-Caselle Airport (TRN) with airlines like British Airways or Ryanair. The flight duration is typically around 2 hours, providing a quick and convenient way to reach Piedmont from the UK.

Alternatively, travelers coming from destinations outside of Europe may opt to fly into Milan Malpensa Airport (MXP), located approximately 120 kilometers southeast of Turin. From Malpensa Airport, you can take advantage of various transportation options, including trains, buses, or rental cars, to reach Piedmont.

Example: If you're traveling from New York City to Piedmont, you can book a flight to Milan Malpensa Airport (MXP) with airlines like Delta Air Lines or Alitalia. The flight duration is approximately 8-9 hours, depending on the airline and routing. Upon arrival at Malpensa Airport, you can take a direct train to Turin or rent a car to explore the region at your leisure.

2. Train:

Italy's extensive rail network makes traveling to Piedmont by train a convenient and scenic option. High-speed trains connect major cities like Milan, Turin, and Genoa to destinations within the region, offering comfortable and efficient transportation for travelers.

Example: Suppose you're traveling from Rome to Turin. You can take a high-speed Frecciarossa train from Roma Termini station to Turin Porta Nuova station. The journey typically takes around 4 hours, allowing you to relax and enjoy the picturesque landscapes of central Italy and the Po Valley along the way.

Once you've arrived in Turin or another major city in Piedmont, you can easily transfer to regional or local trains to reach your final destination within the region. Trains are a popular choice for travelers looking to explore Piedmont's diverse cities, towns, and countryside while avoiding the hassle of driving or navigating unfamiliar roads.

3. Car:

Renting a car gives travelers the flexibility to explore Piedmont at their own pace and on their own schedule. The region is well-connected by highways, making it easy to reach from neighboring countries like France and Switzerland. Driving through Piedmont allows you to discover hidden gems off the beaten path and enjoy the breathtaking landscapes of the Italian Alps.

Example: Suppose you're embarking on a road trip from Geneva, Switzerland, to Piedmont. You can rent a car at Geneva Airport (GVA) and drive southeast through the scenic Mont Blanc Tunnel, crossing into Italy. From there, you can continue your journey through the Aosta Valley and into Piedmont, arriving at destinations like Turin, Aosta, or the Piedmontese Alps.

Upon crossing into Piedmont, travelers are greeted by a tapestry of rolling hills, vineyards, and historic villages waiting to be explored. Driving through the region allows you to stop at your leisure, savoring local delicacies, and soaking in the charm of each unique destination along the way.

Example: As you journey through Piedmont, you might choose to take a scenic drive through the Langhe wine region, renowned for its prestigious Barolo and Barbaresco wines. Along the way, you can visit quaint hilltop towns like La Morra and Barolo, where you can sample world-class wines at local wineries and indulge in Piedmontese cuisine at rustic trattorias.

Renting a car also provides access to remote areas and natural wonders that may not be easily reachable by public transportation. Whether you're seeking the serenity of the Italian countryside, the adrenaline rush of alpine skiing, or the tranquility of Piedmont's picturesque lakes, having a car allows you to tailor your itinerary to your interests and preferences.

Example: If you're a nature enthusiast eager to explore the Gran Paradiso National Park in the Piedmontese Alps. Renting a car allows you to drive to the park's entrance and embark on scenic hikes, spot wildlife, and marvel at towering peaks and cascading waterfalls at your own pace.

While driving in Piedmont offers unparalleled freedom and flexibility, it's essential to familiarize yourself with Italian traffic laws and road signs to ensure a safe and enjoyable journey. Keep in mind that some historic city centers, like Turin's, may have restricted traffic zones (ZTL), where only authorized vehicles are allowed. It's advisable to check with your rental car provider or hotel for guidance on navigating these areas and obtaining necessary permits if needed.

In summary, whether you choose to fly, take the train, or rent a car, getting to Piedmont is a seamless experience with a variety of transportation options to suit every traveler's needs. Once you arrive, exploring the region's diverse landscapes, rich culture, and culinary delights is made easy thanks to its efficient local transportation networks and well-maintained roadways. So pack your bags, embark on your journey to Piedmont, and prepare to be enchanted by all that this captivating region has to offer.

B. International Access Points

Piedmont's strategic location and well-connected transportation infrastructure make it easily accessible from various international points. Whether you're arriving from neighboring European countries or traveling from overseas,

Piedmont offers convenient entry points that cater to a diverse range of travelers.

1. *Turin-Caselle Airport (TRN):*

Located just outside Turin, Turin-Caselle Airport serves as the main international gateway to Piedmont. The airport offers a range of domestic and international flights, making it a convenient entry point for travelers from across Europe and beyond.

Example: Suppose you're traveling from Paris to Piedmont. You can book a direct flight from Paris Charles de Gaulle Airport (CDG) to Turin-Caselle Airport (TRN) with airlines like Air France or EasyJet. The flight duration is approximately 1.5 hours, providing a quick and hassle-free way to reach Piedmont from France.

Upon arrival at Turin-Caselle Airport, travelers can easily access various transportation options, including taxis, shuttle buses, and rental cars, to continue their journey to destinations within

Piedmont. The airport is conveniently located near major highways, allowing for seamless connections to popular tourist destinations such as Turin, Alba, and the Italian Alps.

2. Milan Malpensa Airport (MXP):

While not located within Piedmont itself, Milan Malpensa Airport serves as another major international access point for travelers visiting the region. Situated approximately 120 kilometers southeast of Turin, Malpensa Airport offers a wide range of domestic and international flights, making it a popular choice for travelers coming from overseas.

Example: If you're traveling from New York City to Piedmont, you can book a flight to Milan Malpensa Airport (MXP) with airlines like Delta Air Lines or Alitalia. The flight duration is approximately 8-9 hours, depending on the airline and routing. Upon arrival at Malpensa Airport, travelers can easily transfer to Piedmont via various transportation options, including trains, buses, or rental cars.

From Malpensa Airport, travelers can take advantage of direct train services to Turin or Milan's city centers, where they can then connect to regional train services to reach destinations within Piedmont. Alternatively, rental car facilities are available at the airport for travelers who prefer the flexibility of exploring the region by car.

3. *Milan Linate Airport (LIN):*

Although smaller than Malpensa, Milan Linate Airport offers domestic and international flights, providing another convenient access point for travelers visiting Piedmont. Located approximately 140 kilometers southeast of Turin, Linate Airport is within driving distance of Piedmont's major cities and attractions.

Example: Suppose you're traveling from Munich to Piedmont. You can book a direct flight from Munich Airport (MUC) to Milan Linate Airport

(LIN) with airlines like Lufthansa or Alitalia. The flight duration is typically around 1 hour and 15 minutes, offering a quick and convenient way to reach Piedmont from Germany.

Upon arrival at Linate Airport, travelers can rent a car or take advantage of shuttle buses or taxis to continue their journey to Piedmont. Additionally, regional train services connect Milan's city center to destinations within Piedmont, providing an alternative transportation option for travelers arriving at Linate Airport.

C. Local Transportation Within Piedmont

Once you've arrived in Piedmont, navigating the region's cities, towns, and countryside is made easy thanks to its efficient local transportation network. Whether you're exploring the historic streets of Turin, venturing into the vineyards of Langhe, or relaxing by the shores of Lake Maggiore, Piedmont offers a variety of transportation options to suit every traveler's needs.

1. Train:

Piedmont's rail network provides convenient and reliable transportation between its major cities and towns. Whether you're traveling short distances within a city or embarking on a longer journey between destinations, trains offer a comfortable and scenic way to explore the region.

Example: Suppose you're staying in Turin and want to visit the beautiful town of Alba in the heart of the Langhe wine region. You can take a regional train from Turin Porta Nuova station to Alba station, with a journey time of approximately 1 hour and 30 minutes. Along the way, you'll pass through picturesque countryside, vineyards, and rolling hills, offering glimpses of Piedmont's stunning landscapes.

From major cities like Turin, Asti, and Novara, travelers can access regional and intercity train services that connect Piedmont to other regions of Italy, including Lombardy, Liguria, and

Emilia-Romagna. Whether you're planning a day trip or a longer excursion, trains provide a convenient and environmentally friendly way to travel within Piedmont and beyond.

2. Bus:

Local buses supplement Piedmont's rail network, providing transportation to smaller villages and rural areas not served by trains. Buses offer flexibility and accessibility, allowing travelers to reach destinations off the beaten path and explore Piedmont's hidden gems.

Example: Suppose you're staying in the town of Stresa on the shores of Lake Maggiore and want to explore the nearby Borromean Islands. You can take a local bus from Stresa to the town's ferry terminal, where you can catch a ferry to the islands. The bus journey takes approximately 15 minutes, providing a convenient way to access the ferry services.

In addition to serving rural areas, buses also provide transportation within Piedmont's cities and towns, offering routes that connect key landmarks, attractions, and neighborhoods. Whether you're visiting historic sites, shopping districts, or cultural institutions, buses offer a convenient and cost-effective way to get around.

3. Car Rental:

For travelers seeking flexibility and autonomy, renting a car is an excellent option for exploring Piedmont's diverse landscapes and attractions. Rental agencies are available at major transportation hubs, including airports and train stations, allowing travelers to pick up a vehicle upon arrival and embark on their Piedmont adventure with ease.

Example: Suppose you're staying in the town of Barolo and want to explore the surrounding vineyards and villages at your own pace. You can rent a car from Turin-Caselle Airport or a nearby rental agency and drive to Barolo, enjoying the freedom to stop and explore charming towns like La Morra and Monforte d'Alba along the way.

Having a car allows travelers to venture off the beaten path, discover hidden treasures, and immerse themselves in Piedmont's rich culture and natural beauty. Whether you're exploring the rolling hills of the Langhe, the rugged peaks of the Alps, or the tranquil countryside, a car provides the freedom to create your own itinerary and experience Piedmont on your terms.

Chapter 3: Top Destinations in Piedmont

Piedmont, with its rich history, stunning landscapes, and delectable cuisine, offers a myriad of captivating destinations for travelers to explore. From vibrant cities to serene countryside retreats, the region boasts something for every type of traveler. In this chapter, we will delve into some of the top destinations that should not be missed during your visit to Piedmont.

A. Turin (Torino)

Nestled amidst the stunning backdrop of the Alps, Turin, or Torino as it's known in Italian, stands as a cultural gem in the heart of Piedmont. With a history dating back to Roman times, this vibrant city boasts a wealth of architectural marvels, world-class museums, and culinary delights that entice travelers from around the globe.

History and Architecture

Turin's rich history is reflected in its impressive array of architectural treasures. From the grandeur of the Royal Palace of Turin to the iconic Mole Antonelliana, the city is a testament to its royal past and cultural heritage. The Royal Palace, once home to the House of Savoy, offers visitors a glimpse into the lavish lifestyle of Italy's former rulers, with opulent halls, magnificent gardens, and priceless artworks.

The Mole Antonelliana, towering over the city skyline, serves as a symbol of Turin and houses the National Cinema Museum, where visitors can explore the fascinating history of Italian cinema and enjoy panoramic views of the city from its observation deck.

Culture and Museums

Turin is a haven for art and culture enthusiasts, with a plethora of museums and galleries waiting to be explored. The Egyptian Museum, the largest collection of Egyptian artifacts outside of Cairo, is a must-visit for history buffs, while the GAM - Gallery of Modern Art showcases an impressive collection of contemporary artworks spanning the 19th and 20th centuries.

For those interested in automotive history, the Museo Nazionale dell'Automobile offers a fascinating journey through the evolution of Italian car design, with iconic models from manufacturers such as Fiat, Alfa Romeo, and Ferrari on display.

Culinary Delights

No visit to Turin would be complete without indulging in its culinary delights. The city is renowned for its chocolate and coffee culture, with historic cafes such as Caffè Mulassano and Caffè Al Bicerin serving up decadent treats that have been delighting locals and visitors alike for centuries.

Turin is also famous for its aperitivo tradition, where bars and cafes offer complimentary snacks to accompany your pre-dinner drinks. Sample local specialties such as vitello tonnato (veal with tuna sauce), agnolotti del plin (filled pasta parcels), and bicerin (a traditional coffee drink layered with chocolate and cream) as you soak in the city's vibrant atmosphere.

Outdoor Attractions

Despite its urban setting, Turin offers plenty of opportunities to enjoy the great outdoors. The Parco del Valentino, located along the banks of the Po River, is the perfect place to escape the hustle and bustle of the city and unwind amidst lush greenery and scenic views.

For those seeking adventure, the nearby Alps provide ample opportunities for hiking, skiing, and other outdoor activities year-round. With its perfect blend of history, culture, and natural beauty, Turin truly offers something for every traveler to discover and enjoy.

B. Alba

Tucked away in the rolling hills of the Langhe region, Alba exudes charm and character, captivating visitors with its quaint streets, historic landmarks, and culinary delights. Renowned as the gastronomic capital of Piedmont, this picturesque town is a haven for food enthusiasts, with its truffles, hazelnuts, and exquisite wines drawing visitors from far and wide.

Truffle Capital

Alba's claim to fame lies in its coveted white truffles, often referred to as "diamonds of the kitchen." Every autumn, the town comes alive with the annual International White Truffle Fair, where visitors can sample and purchase these prized delicacies from local truffle hunters and vendors. Indulge in truffle-infused dishes at the town's restaurants, or embark on a truffle hunting excursion in the surrounding countryside for a truly immersive experience.

Historic Landmarks

Steeped in history, Alba boasts a wealth of historic landmarks waiting to be explored. The medieval towers that dot the skyline, such as the Torre dell'Orologio and the Torre Comunale, offer panoramic views of the surrounding countryside and provide a glimpse into the town's storied past.

The Cathedral of San Lorenzo, with its ornate façade and beautiful frescoes, is another must-visit attraction, showcasing the rich architectural heritage of the region. Stroll through the charming streets of the old town, lined with centuries-old buildings and charming piazzas, and soak in the timeless atmosphere of this medieval gem.

Culinary Delights

In addition to its truffles, Alba is also renowned for its hazelnuts and exquisite wines. Sample locally produced hazelnut products, from creamy gianduja chocolate to fragrant hazelnut liqueurs, at specialty shops and artisanal producers scattered throughout the town.

Wine enthusiasts will delight in exploring the surrounding vineyards and wineries, where they can taste the region's famous Barbaresco and Barolo wines. Join a guided wine tour to learn about the winemaking process and discover the unique terroir that gives Piedmont wines their distinctive flavor profiles.

Festivals and Events

Throughout the year, Alba hosts a variety of festivals and events that celebrate its rich cultural heritage and culinary traditions. From the Alba White Truffle Fair to the Vinum wine festival, there's always something exciting happening in town.

Don't miss the annual Palio degli Asini, a traditional donkey race held in the historic city center, where locals and visitors alike gather to cheer on their favorite teams and enjoy the festive atmosphere. Whether you're a food lover, history buff, or simply seeking a charming getaway, Alba offers an unforgettable experience that will leave you longing to return.

C. Asti

Nestled amidst the rolling hills of the Piedmontese countryside, Asti enchants visitors with its medieval charm, lively festivals, and world-renowned wines. As one of the region's oldest cities, Asti boasts a rich history dating back to Roman times, with its well-preserved historic center serving as a testament to its storied past.

Palio di Asti

One of the highlights of the Asti calendar is the Palio di Asti, a traditional bareback horse race that dates back to the 13th century. Held annually in September, this thrilling event sees riders from the city's historic neighborhoods competing for glory in a series of adrenaline-fueled races around the central Piazza Alfieri. The Palio is accompanied by colorful parades, flag-throwing competitions, and medieval reenactments, making it a must-see spectacle for visitors to Asti.

Historic Landmarks

Asti is home to a wealth of historic landmarks that offer insight into the city's rich cultural heritage. The towering Torre Troyana, part of the medieval city walls, offers panoramic views of the surrounding countryside and serves as a reminder of Asti's medieval glory days. The Cathedral of Santa Maria Assunta, with its stunning Gothic façade and ornate interior, is another must-visit attraction, housing priceless artworks and religious relics.

Stroll through the atmospheric streets of the old town, lined with ancient palaces, charming piazzas, and bustling markets, and soak in the timeless beauty of this historic city.

Sparkling Wines

Asti is famous for its sparkling wines, particularly Asti Spumante, a sweet and aromatic sparkling wine made from Moscato grapes. Visitors can explore the city's many wineries and cellars, where they can sample a wide variety of wines and learn about the traditional methods used to produce them.

Be sure to visit during the annual Douja d'Or wine competition, held in September, where the region's finest wines are showcased and celebrated. Whether you're a wine connoisseur or simply appreciate a good glass of bubbly, Asti offers plenty of opportunities to indulge in the local wine culture.

Gastronomic Delights

In addition to its wines, Asti is also renowned for its delicious cuisine, with local specialties ranging from hearty meat dishes to delicate pastries. Sample traditional dishes such as bagna cauda (a warm anchovy and garlic dip served with vegetables), agnolotti del plin (filled pasta parcels), and brasato al Barbera (beef braised in Barbera wine) at one of the city's many trattorias and osterias.

Save room for dessert and indulge in sweet treats like amaretti (almond cookies) and torta di nocciole (hazelnut cake), made with the region's famous Tonda Gentile delle Langhe hazelnuts. With its rich culinary heritage and vibrant atmosphere, Asti promises a feast for the senses that will leave you craving more.

D. Lake Maggiore

Nestled amidst the breathtaking scenery of the Italian Alps, Lake Maggiore is a picturesque destination that captivates visitors with its crystal-clear waters, lush gardens, and charming lakeside towns. Stretching from Italy into Switzerland, this expansive lake offers a wealth of opportunities for relaxation, exploration, and outdoor adventure.

Scenic Beauty

Surrounded by snow-capped mountains and verdant hillsides, Lake Maggiore boasts some of the most stunning scenery in Italy. Take a leisurely boat cruise along the lake's tranquil waters and soak in the breathtaking views of the surrounding landscape, dotted with quaint villages, historic castles, and lush gardens.

Visit the Borromean Islands, a group of picturesque islands located in the middle of the lake, where you can explore ornate palaces, manicured gardens, and exotic plants from around the world. Don't miss the stunning Isola Bella, with its magnificent Baroque palace and terraced gardens cascading down to the water's edge.

Outdoor Activities

Lake Maggiore offers plenty of opportunities for outdoor adventure and recreation. Explore the scenic hiking trails that wind their way through the surrounding mountains and forests, offering panoramic views of the lake and beyond. Cyclists will delight in the network of cycling paths that crisscross the region, providing a scenic way to explore the countryside.

Water sports enthusiasts can enjoy a variety of activities on the lake, including swimming, sailing, kayaking, and windsurfing. Fishing enthusiasts can try their luck in the lake's clear waters, which are home to a variety of fish species, including trout, pike, and perch.

Lakeside Towns

The charming lakeside towns that dot the shores of Lake Maggiore offer a glimpse into traditional Italian life and culture. Explore picturesque towns such as Stresa, with its elegant promenade, historic villas, and bustling markets, or Verbania, home to the stunning Villa Taranto botanical gardens.

Visit the town of Cannobio, with its charming old town and lively waterfront, or venture further afield to the Swiss town of Locarno, where you can explore historic churches, stroll along the lakeside promenade, and take in panoramic views from the nearby mountains.

Cultural Attractions

Lake Maggiore is also home to a variety of cultural attractions and historic landmarks. Visit the Rocca di Angera, a medieval fortress perched high above the lake, where you can explore ancient ruins, climb the tower for panoramic views, and visit the fascinating Doll and Toy Museum housed within its walls.

Explore the charming villages of the Cannobina Valley, with their traditional stone houses and narrow cobblestone streets, or visit the picturesque town of Orta San Giulio, located on the shores of nearby Lake Orta, with its charming medieval buildings and stunning island monastery.

Whether you're seeking relaxation, adventure, or cultural enrichment, Lake Maggiore offers a wealth of experiences that will leave you enchanted and inspired.

E. Langhe Wine Region

Nestled amidst the rolling hills of southern Piedmont, the Langhe wine region is a paradise for wine enthusiasts and nature lovers alike. Renowned for its picturesque vineyards, charming hilltop villages, and world-class wines, this idyllic countryside destination offers a quintessential Italian experience that is sure to enchant visitors.

Vineyard Landscape

The Langhe region's stunning landscape is dominated by vine-covered hillsides that stretch as far as the eye can see. The unique terroir of the area, characterized by its limestone-rich soil and mild climate, provides the perfect conditions for cultivating grapes, particularly the Nebbiolo grape used to produce the region's famous Barolo and Barbaresco wines.

Take a scenic drive along the Strada del Barolo, winding through picturesque villages and vineyards, and stop at local wineries to taste the region's finest wines and learn about the winemaking process from passionate producers.

Hilltop Villages

The Langhe region is dotted with charming hilltop villages that seem frozen in time, with their narrow cobblestone streets, medieval towers, and ancient churches. Explore quaint villages such as Barolo, La Morra, and Serralunga d'Alba, each boasting its own unique charm and character.

Wander through the historic streets, browse artisan shops and boutiques, and soak in the panoramic views of the surrounding countryside from the village's highest vantage points. Don't miss the opportunity to dine at a local trattoria or osteria, where you can savor traditional Piedmontese dishes paired with the region's finest wines.

Culinary Delights

In addition to its world-class wines, the Langhe region is also renowned for its delicious cuisine, with local specialties ranging from hearty meat dishes to delicate pastas and decadent desserts. Sample traditional dishes such as tajarin al tartufo (fresh pasta with shaved truffles), bagna cauda (a warm anchovy and garlic dip served with vegetables), and brasato al Barolo (beef braised in Barolo wine) at one of the region's many charming restaurants and agriturismi.

Save room for dessert and indulge in sweet treats like hazelnut cake, panna cotta, and gianduja chocolate, made with the region's famous Tonda Gentile delle Langhe hazelnuts. With its rich culinary heritage and emphasis on locally sourced ingredients, the Langhe region promises a gastronomic journey that will delight and satisfy even the most discerning palate.

Outdoor Activities

The Langhe region offers plenty of opportunities for outdoor adventure and exploration. Lace up your hiking boots and explore the network of scenic hiking trails that wind their way through the vineyards and forests, offering breathtaking views of the surrounding countryside.

Cycling enthusiasts can explore the region's picturesque countryside on two wheels, following dedicated cycling routes such as the Langhe Monferrato Roero Wine Route, which takes cyclists on a scenic journey through the heart of Piedmont's wine country.

Whether you're a wine lover, foodie, or outdoor enthusiast, the Langhe wine region offers a wealth of experiences that will leave you enchanted and eager to return.

F. Barolo Wine Region

Nestled amidst the rolling hills of the Langhe region, the Barolo wine region is synonymous with luxury, elegance, and world-class wine. Home to the prestigious Barolo wine, often referred to as the "king of wines," this picturesque countryside destination offers visitors a glimpse into the rich winemaking tradition of Piedmont and a chance to taste some of Italy's finest wines.

Barolo Wine

The Barolo wine region is famous for its eponymous wine, made from the Nebbiolo grape grown in the surrounding vineyards. Known for its complex flavors, rich aromas, and ability to age gracefully, Barolo wine is considered one of Italy's greatest red wines and is highly sought after by wine enthusiasts around the world.

Visit local wineries and cellars to taste a variety of Barolo wines, from traditional to modern styles, and learn about the unique terroir and winemaking techniques that give each wine its distinctive character. Don't miss the opportunity to explore the Barolo Wine Museum, located in the historic Castle of Barolo, where you can learn about the history and culture of this iconic wine.

Picturesque Vineyards

The Barolo wine region is characterized by its picturesque vineyards, which blanket the rolling hillsides in a patchwork of colors throughout the year. Take a leisurely drive or bike ride along the scenic wine routes that wind their way through the countryside, offering panoramic views of the vineyards and surrounding landscape.

Stop at local vineyards and wineries along the way to sample the region's wines and enjoy guided tours and tastings led by knowledgeable winemakers. Whether you're a seasoned oenophile or a casual wine lover, exploring the vineyards of the Barolo wine region is sure to be a memorable experience.

Charming Villages

The Barolo wine region is dotted with charming villages and towns that seem frozen in time, with their narrow cobblestone streets, historic churches, and medieval castles. Explore picturesque villages such as Barolo, La Morra, and Monforte d'Alba, each boasting its own unique charm and character.

Wander through the historic streets, browse artisan shops and boutiques, and soak in the breathtaking views of the surrounding countryside from the village's highest vantage points. Don't miss the opportunity to dine at a local trattoria or osteria, where you can savor traditional Piedmontese dishes paired with the region's finest wines.

Cultural Heritage

In addition to its wine, the Barolo wine region is also rich in cultural heritage, with historic landmarks and attractions waiting to be explored. Visit the Castle of Barolo, home to the Barolo Wine Museum and surrounded by vineyards, where you can learn about the history and production of Barolo wine.

Explore the charming villages of the region, with their ancient churches, medieval towers, and quaint piazzas, or venture further afield to nearby towns such as Alba and Asti, where you can immerse yourself in the rich history and culture of

Piedmont. Whether you're a wine enthusiast, history buff, or simply seeking a tranquil retreat amidst the vineyards, the Barolo wine region offers a truly unforgettable experience that will leave you longing to return.

In the heart of Piedmont, these top destinations promise an enriching travel experience, where history, culture, and gastronomy converge to create unforgettable memories amidst Italy's northern gem. Whether exploring vibrant cities, tranquil lakeshores, or renowned wine regions, Piedmont captivates the soul and ignites the spirit of adventure.

Chapter 4: Activities and Attractions

Piedmont offers an abundance of activities and attractions that cater to every traveler's interests. From outdoor adventures to historical landmarks, culinary delights, and vibrant festivals, there is something for everyone to enjoy in this diverse region of Italy.

A. Outdoor Activities

Piedmont's rugged terrain and diverse landscapes make it an ideal destination for outdoor enthusiasts seeking adventure and natural beauty. From the majestic peaks of the Alps to the rolling hills of the Langhe and Monferrato wine regions, there are countless opportunities for exploration and outdoor recreation.

Hiking

Hiking is a popular activity in Piedmont, offering travelers the chance to immerse themselves in the region's stunning scenery while enjoying fresh air and exercise. The area is crisscrossed with a network of well-marked trails that cater to hikers of all skill levels, from gentle strolls through vineyards to challenging treks in the mountains.

One of the most iconic hiking destinations in Piedmont is the Gran Paradiso National Park, home to towering peaks, alpine meadows, and abundant wildlife. Here, visitors can embark on multi-day treks or shorter day hikes, taking in panoramic views of glaciers, valleys, and pristine alpine lakes along the way.

Closer to the city of Turin, the Superga Basilica offers a scenic starting point for hikes up the Superga Hill, where sweeping vistas of the city and surrounding countryside await. For those seeking a more leisurely experience, the vineyard-covered hills of the Langhe offer picturesque trails that wind through charming villages and rolling countryside, providing ample opportunities to sample local wines along the way.

Skiing

In the winter months, Piedmont transforms into a winter wonderland, attracting skiing and snowboarding enthusiasts from around the world. The region is home to several world-class ski resorts, including Sestriere, Bardonecchia, and Limone Piemonte, offering a variety of terrain for skiers of all levels.

Sestriere, part of the expansive Via Lattea (Milky Way) ski area, hosted the alpine events during the 2006 Winter Olympics and boasts over 400 kilometers of interconnected slopes and modern lift systems. Whether carving down groomed runs, tackling off-piste terrain, or practicing tricks in terrain parks, visitors will find plenty of options for snowy fun in Piedmont's ski resorts.

For those seeking a more serene experience, cross-country skiing and snowshoeing are popular activities in the region, with numerous trails winding through snow-covered forests and alpine meadows. Guided tours and equipment rentals are available for visitors looking to explore the winter wonderland of Piedmont at a slower pace.

Cycling

With its gently rolling hills, scenic countryside, and well-maintained roads, Piedmont is a cyclist's paradise. The region offers a variety of cycling routes, from leisurely rides through vineyards and orchards to challenging climbs in the Alps.

One of the most popular cycling destinations in Piedmont is the Langhe wine region, where cyclists can pedal along winding roads that meander through picturesque villages, rolling hills, and vineyard-covered slopes. Along the way, cyclists can stop at local wineries to sample award-winning Barolo and Barbaresco wines, as well as indulge in the region's culinary delights.

For more adventurous cyclists, the Alps provide a dramatic backdrop for challenging rides and epic climbs. The Colle delle Finestre, Colle del Nivolet, and Colle del Moncenisio are just a few of the legendary mountain passes that attract cyclists seeking the ultimate test of endurance and skill.

Whether exploring the countryside on two wheels, hitting the slopes in winter, or trekking through alpine landscapes, outdoor enthusiasts will find endless opportunities for adventure and exploration in Piedmont's breathtaking natural surroundings.

B. Historical Landmarks and Museums

Piedmont is steeped in history, with a wealth of historical landmarks and museums that offer insight into the region's rich cultural heritage. From ancient Roman ruins to majestic royal palaces, visitors can step back in time and explore centuries of history in Piedmont's charming towns and cities.

Turin: The Royal City

The city of Turin, Piedmont's capital, is a treasure trove of historical landmarks and architectural wonders. At the heart of the city stands the magnificent Palazzo Reale (Royal Palace), once the seat of the House of Savoy, Italy's ruling dynasty for over seven centuries. Visitors can explore opulent state apartments, royal gardens, and the stunning Royal Armoury, home to one of Europe's most impressive collections of arms and armor.

Nearby, the Palazzo Madama houses the Turin City Museum of Ancient Art, showcasing masterpieces from antiquity to the Renaissance period, while the Mole Antonelliana, an iconic symbol of the city, houses the National Museum of Cinema, where visitors can explore the history of film through interactive exhibits and screenings.

Sacri Monti: Sacred Mountains

Piedmont is home to the Sacri Monti (Sacred Mountains), a series of nine UNESCO World Heritage sites that dot the landscape of the region. These picturesque complexes of chapels and shrines were built between the 16th and 17th centuries as expressions of religious devotion and feature stunning frescoes, sculptures, and architectural details.

One of the most famous Sacri Monti is located in the town of Varallo Sesia, where the Sacro Monte di Varallo offers visitors a spiritual journey through the life of Christ, depicted in a series of 45 chapels set amidst a scenic natural setting. Other notable Sacri Monti include those in Oropa, Orta San Giulio, and Crea, each offering a unique blend of art, history, and spirituality.

Medieval Towns and Castles

Piedmont is dotted with charming medieval towns and villages, where visitors can wander through narrow cobblestone streets, admire ancient architecture, and soak in the atmosphere of centuries past. The town of Alba, known for its truffles and hazelnuts, boasts a picturesque historic center dotted with medieval towers and Renaissance palaces.

In the town of Ivrea, visitors can explore the imposing ruins of the Ivrea Castle, once a stronghold of the House of Savoy, while the nearby town of Saluzzo is home to a well-preserved medieval old town, complete with ancient palaces, churches, and fortified walls.

Ancient Roman Ruins

Piedmont's history dates back to ancient times, and evidence of its Roman past can be found scattered throughout the region. The city of Aosta, located in the Aosta Valley region of Piedmont, is home to some of the best-preserved Roman ruins in Italy, including the imposing Arch of Augustus and the well-preserved Roman Theatre.

Outside of Aosta, visitors can explore the ruins of the Roman city of Augusta Taurinorum, modern-day Turin, where ancient walls, amphitheaters, and thermal baths offer a glimpse into the daily life of Roman settlers in Piedmont.

From grand palaces and medieval towns to ancient ruins and sacred mountains, Piedmont's historical landmarks and museums offer travelers a fascinating journey through the region's rich and diverse history. Whether exploring ancient Roman sites, admiring Baroque architecture, or delving into religious art, visitors will find endless opportunities to uncover the secrets of Piedmont's past.

C. Culinary Experiences

Piedmont is renowned for its exquisite cuisine, which reflects the region's rich agricultural heritage and culinary traditions. From hearty mountain fare to delicate pastries and fine wines, visitors can indulge in a diverse array of culinary delights that showcase the best of Piedmont's gastronomic offerings.

Truffles and Tartufi

Piedmont is famous for its truffles, particularly the prized white truffle or "tartufo bianco," which is considered one of the most sought-after delicacies in the world. The town of Alba, in the heart of the Langhe region, is renowned for its annual White Truffle Fair, where visitors can sample freshly harvested truffles and attend truffle auctions, cooking demonstrations, and tasting events.

Truffle hunting tours offer a unique opportunity to experience the thrill of searching for these elusive fungi alongside expert truffle hunters and their trusty truffle-hunting dogs. Guided tours typically include a walk through the forest, followed by a truffle-themed lunch featuring dishes such as tajarin pasta with shaved truffles, risotto al tartufo, and truffle-infused cheeses.

Wine Tasting in the Langhe

Piedmont is also celebrated for its prestigious wine regions, particularly the Langhe, home to renowned red wines such as Barolo and Barbaresco. Wine enthusiasts can embark on guided wine tours and tastings at family-owned wineries and historic estates, where they can sample a variety of vintages and learn about the region's winemaking traditions from knowledgeable sommeliers and winemakers.

Visitors can explore the picturesque vineyard landscapes of the Langhe by car, bicycle, or on foot, stopping at wineries along the way to taste Nebbiolo, Barbera, Dolcetto, and other local varietals. Many wineries offer cellar tours and wine-pairing experiences, allowing guests to savor the flavors of Piedmontese cuisine alongside their favorite wines.

Piedmontese Cuisine

Piedmontese cuisine is known for its emphasis on simple, high-quality ingredients and rich, hearty flavors. Signature dishes include "vitello tonnato," thinly sliced veal served with a creamy tuna sauce; "agnolotti del plin," small pockets of pasta stuffed with meat or vegetables; and "bagna cauda," a warm anchovy and garlic dip served with raw vegetables.

Visitors can sample these and other traditional Piedmontese dishes at local trattorias, osterias, and agriturismi, where farm-fresh ingredients are transformed into delicious regional specialties. Cooking classes offer a hands-on opportunity to learn the secrets of Piedmontese cuisine from local chefs, who share their favorite recipes and techniques for preparing classic dishes.

Chocolate and Gelato

Piedmont is also famous for its chocolate and gelato, with the city of Turin earning a reputation as Italy's chocolate capital. Visitors can indulge their sweet tooth with a visit to historic chocolate shops such as Baratti & Milano and Guido Gobino, where they can sample decadent gianduja chocolates, creamy pralines, and other confections made with locally sourced hazelnuts.

Gelato aficionados will find no shortage of artisanal gelaterias offering a tantalizing array of flavors, from classic favorites like stracciatella and pistachio to innovative combinations featuring seasonal fruits and regional ingredients. Whether enjoyed as a refreshing treat on a hot summer day or a decadent dessert after a meal, Piedmontese gelato is sure to delight visitors of all ages.

From truffle hunts and wine tastings to cooking classes and chocolate tours, Piedmont offers a feast for the senses that celebrates the region's culinary heritage and gastronomic delights. Whether savoring the flavors of a traditional Piedmontese meal or indulging in sweet treats and fine wines, visitors are sure to create unforgettable culinary memories in this food lover's paradise.

With its blend of natural beauty, rich history, exquisite cuisine, and vibrant culture, Piedmont invites travelers to embark on a journey of discovery and exploration. Whether you're seeking adventure in the great outdoors or craving a taste of authentic Italian hospitality, Piedmont promises an unforgettable experience that will leave a lasting impression.

Chapter 5: Accommodation Options

Finding the perfect place to stay during your travels is essential for a memorable experience in Piedmont. Whether you prefer the luxury of hotels, the charm of bed and breakfasts, the authenticity of agriturismo, or the flexibility of rental apartments/houses, Piedmont offers a wide range of accommodation options to suit every traveler's needs and preferences.

A. Hotels

Hotels in Piedmont encompass a wide spectrum of styles, sizes, and amenities, catering to the diverse needs and preferences of travelers. From luxurious five-star establishments to budget-friendly options, there's something for every type of visitor.

Luxury Hotels:

For those seeking indulgence and opulence, Piedmont boasts several prestigious luxury hotels renowned for their exquisite accommodations, impeccable service, and world-class amenities. Examples include:

- ***Castello di Guarene:*** Situated in a beautifully restored 18th-century castle near Alba, this luxury hotel offers panoramic views of the surrounding vineyards and countryside. Guests can enjoy luxurious suites, Michelin-starred dining, a spa, and access to nearby golf courses and wineries.

- ***Relais San Maurizio:*** Nestled in the hills of the Langhe region, this former 17th-century monastery has been transformed into an elegant luxury hotel and spa. Guests can relax in spacious rooms and suites adorned with antique furnishings, dine at the gourmet restaurant, and unwind in the wellness center featuring a Turkish bath, sauna, and indoor pool.

Boutique Hotels:

Piedmont is dotted with charming boutique hotels, each offering a unique blend of style, character, and personalized service. These intimate properties provide an authentic and immersive experience for discerning travelers. Examples include:

- *Villa Crespi:* Located on the shores of Lake Orta, Villa Crespi is a Moorish-inspired mansion built in the late 19th century. This boutique hotel features luxurious rooms and suites adorned with ornate décor, a two-Michelin-starred restaurant serving innovative Mediterranean cuisine, and a tranquil garden overlooking the lake.

- *Cascina Barac:* Set amidst the rolling hills of Monferrato, Cascina Barac is a boutique hotel housed in a restored farmhouse dating back to the 18th century. Guests can enjoy elegantly appointed rooms, a charming courtyard garden, and personalized hospitality, including wine tastings and cooking classes showcasing Piedmontese cuisine.

Budget-Friendly Options:

Travelers on a budget will find plenty of affordable hotel options in Piedmont, providing comfortable accommodations without breaking the bank. These budget-friendly hotels offer convenient locations and essential amenities for a pleasant stay. Examples include:

- *Hotel Diplomatic:* Situated in the heart of Turin, Hotel Diplomatic offers clean and comfortable rooms at an affordable price. Guests can enjoy complimentary breakfast, free Wi-Fi, and easy access to the city's main attractions, including the Egyptian Museum and Mole Antonelliana.

- *Hotel Langhe:* Located in the town of Alba, Hotel Langhe provides budget-friendly accommodation near the historic city center. The hotel features simple yet cozy rooms, a bar, and a restaurant serving traditional Piedmontese dishes, making it an ideal choice for travelers exploring the region on a budget.

Whether you're seeking luxury, boutique charm, or affordability, Piedmont's diverse selection of hotels ensures that every traveler finds the perfect place to stay during their visit to this enchanting region.

B. Bed and Breakfasts

Bed and breakfasts offer a unique and intimate accommodation experience, providing travelers with a cozy home away from home. Piedmont's picturesque villages and countryside are dotted with charming B&Bs, each offering warm hospitality, personalized service, and a glimpse into local life.

Historic Residences:
Many bed and breakfasts in Piedmont are housed in historic buildings, ranging from ancient palaces to renovated farmhouses, adding to their charm and character. Guests can immerse themselves in the region's rich history while enjoying modern comforts and amenities. Examples include:

- ***Casa dei Nonni:*** Located in the historic center of Barolo, Casa dei Nonni is a charming B&B housed in a 19th-century building overlooking the vineyards of the Langhe region. Guests can stay in beautifully appointed rooms with traditional décor, savor homemade breakfasts featuring local specialties, and explore the nearby wineries and medieval villages.

- ***Villa Morneto:*** Situated amidst the rolling hills of Monferrato, Villa Morneto is a historic estate dating back to the 16th century. This elegant B&B offers spacious rooms and suites with antique furnishings, a lush garden with panoramic views, and a swimming pool for guests to relax and unwind.

Family-Run Establishments:
Many bed and breakfasts in Piedmont are family-run, providing guests with personalized attention and insider recommendations for exploring the region. These cozy accommodations offer a warm and welcoming atmosphere, making

guests feel like part of the family. Examples include:

- **La Corte del Barbio:** Nestled in the village of Neive, La Corte del Barbio is a family-run B&B housed in a traditional Piedmontese farmhouse. Guests can enjoy comfortable rooms decorated with rustic charm, homemade breakfasts prepared with ingredients from the family's garden, and friendly hospitality from the owners, who are passionate about sharing their love for Piedmont.

- **Cascina La Barba:** Located in the heart of the Roero wine region, Cascina La Barba is a family-owned B&B surrounded by vineyards and hazelnut orchards. Guests can relax in cozy rooms with panoramic views, dine on farm-to-table meals prepared by the owners, and participate in wine tastings and cooking classes showcasing local ingredients and traditions.

Rural Retreats:
Bed and breakfasts in rural Piedmont offer guests a peaceful retreat away from the hustle and bustle of

city life. Surrounded by nature and countryside vistas, these accommodations provide the perfect setting for relaxation and rejuvenation. Examples include:

- ***Ca' San Sebastiano:*** Tucked away in the hills of Monferrato, Ca' San Sebastiano is a tranquil B&B housed in a restored farmhouse overlooking vineyards and rolling hills. Guests can unwind in spacious rooms with exposed beams and stone walls, enjoy breakfast on the terrace with panoramic views, and explore the surrounding countryside on foot or by bike.

- ***Cascina Sant'Antonio:*** Set amidst the vineyards of the Langhe region, Cascina Sant'Antonio is a rustic B&B offering a peaceful retreat surrounded by nature. Guests can stay in cozy rooms with countryside views, relax in the garden with a glass of local wine, and take leisurely walks through the nearby vineyards and forests.

Whether you're seeking history, family warmth, or rural tranquility, Piedmont's bed and breakfasts provide a cozy and authentic accommodation experience that allows guests to immerse themselves in the region's culture, cuisine, and natural beauty.

C. Agriturismo (Farm Stays)

Immerse yourself in Piedmont's rural charm and agricultural traditions by staying at an agriturismo, where you can experience firsthand the beauty of farm life and savor the flavors of the land. These unique accommodations offer a blend of rustic charm, farm-to-table cuisine, and outdoor activities, providing guests with an authentic taste of Piedmontese culture.

Vineyard Estates:
Piedmont is renowned for its world-class wines, and many agriturismi are located on vineyard estates, allowing guests to explore the winemaking process and sample the region's finest vintages. Guests can participate in vineyard tours, wine tastings, and cellar visits, gaining insight into the art and science of winemaking. Examples include:

- *Agriturismo La Raia:* Situated in the Gavi wine region, Agriturismo La Raia is a sustainable farm and winery producing organic wines and cultivating biodynamic vineyards. Guests can stay in beautifully restored farmhouses, dine on farm-to-table meals prepared with organic ingredients, and enjoy wine tastings overlooking the vineyards.

- *Azienda Agricola Fontanabianca:* Nestled in the heart of the Langhe region, Azienda Agricola Fontanabianca is a family-owned winery and agriturismo producing Barolo and Barbera wines. Guests can stay in cozy rooms overlooking the vineyards, participate in guided wine tastings and vineyard walks, and learn about the winemaking process from the owners.

Farmhouse Retreats:
Experience the rustic beauty of Piedmont's countryside by staying at a farmhouse agriturismo, where guests can enjoy peaceful surroundings, farm-fresh meals, and outdoor activities. These

family-run establishments offer a warm and welcoming atmosphere, making guests feel like part of the farm family. Examples include:

- **Agriturismo Cascina Barisel:** Located in the Alta Langa area, Agriturismo Cascina Barisel is a working farm producing organic fruits, vegetables, and hazelnuts. Guests can stay in comfortable rooms furnished with traditional décor, dine on home-cooked meals prepared with farm-fresh ingredients, and participate in agricultural activities such as fruit picking and hazelnut harvesting.

- **Agriturismo Ca' del Lupo:** Perched on a hilltop overlooking the Roero wine region, Agriturismo Ca' del Lupo is a charming farmhouse offering panoramic views of the surrounding countryside. Guests can relax in cozy rooms decorated with rustic furnishings, dine on Piedmontese specialties at the onsite restaurant, and explore the farm's olive groves, vineyards, and gardens.

Country Retreats:

Escape the hustle and bustle of city life by staying at a countryside agriturismo, where guests can enjoy peace, tranquility, and breathtaking views of Piedmont's landscapes. These secluded retreats offer a perfect setting for relaxation, outdoor activities, and reconnecting with nature. Examples include:

- *Agriturismo Tenuta Carretta:* Situated in the rolling hills of the Roero wine region, Agriturismo Tenuta Carretta is a historic estate surrounded by vineyards and forests. Guests can stay in elegantly appointed rooms and suites, dine on gourmet cuisine at the onsite restaurant, and explore the estate's hiking trails, gardens, and wine cellar.

- *Agriturismo Il Cascinale Nuovo:* Located near the town of Acqui Terme, Agriturismo Il Cascinale Nuovo is a peaceful retreat set amidst vineyards and olive groves. Guests can relax in cozy rooms with rustic décor, swim in the outdoor pool, and enjoy leisurely walks through the surrounding countryside.

Whether you're interested in wine tasting, farm-to-table dining, or simply unwinding in nature, Piedmont's agriturismi offer a unique and immersive accommodation experience that allows guests to connect with the land, the people, and the traditions of this enchanting region.

With its diverse range of accommodation options, Piedmont caters to travelers of all tastes and preferences, ensuring a memorable and enjoyable stay in this captivating region of Italy. Choose the accommodation that best suits your needs and embark on an unforgettable journey filled with culture, cuisine, and scenic beauty.

Chapter 6: Dining and Cuisine

Piedmont, renowned for its culinary excellence, offers a tantalizing array of traditional dishes, Michelin-starred restaurants, cozy trattorias, and bustling food markets. Delve into the rich gastronomic heritage of the region as you explore its diverse flavors and culinary treasures.

A. Traditional Piedmontese Dishes

Piedmontese cuisine is a harmonious blend of rustic simplicity and refined elegance, drawing inspiration from the region's bountiful harvests and centuries-old culinary traditions. Here, we delve into the heart of Piedmont's gastronomic heritage, exploring traditional dishes that embody the essence of this beloved Italian region.

Examples of Traditional Piedmontese Dishes:

1. Bagna Cauda:

Description: Bagna Cauda, literally translating to "hot bath," is a quintessential Piedmontese dish featuring a warm, savory dip made with garlic, anchovies, olive oil, and sometimes butter. It is typically served with a variety of fresh, crisp vegetables such as bell peppers, fennel, carrots, and celery.

Exploration Tip: * Experience the authentic preparation of Bagna Cauda by participating in a cooking class led by a local chef. Learn the secrets behind this beloved dish while enjoying the convivial atmosphere of a traditional Piedmontese kitchen.

2. Tajarin al Tartufo:

Description: Tajarin are thin, delicate egg noodles that are a staple in Piedmontese cuisine. When paired with the region's prized truffles, they become a culinary masterpiece known as Tajarin al Tartufo. This dish showcases the earthy aroma and exquisite flavor of fresh truffles, which are shaved generously over the pasta and typically tossed with butter or cream sauce.

Exploration Tip: Indulge in a truffle hunting excursion in the picturesque hills of Langhe or Roero. Accompanied by a knowledgeable truffle hunter and their trusty dog, embark on a quest to unearth these elusive gems before enjoying a decadent meal featuring Tajarin al Tartufo.

3. Vitello Tonnato:

Description: Vitello Tonnato is a classic Piedmontese antipasto consisting of thinly sliced, tender veal smothered in a velvety tuna and caper sauce. The combination of flavors—savory meat, tangy sauce, and briny capers—creates a harmonious balance that delights the palate.

Exploration Tip: Visit a traditional trattoria or osteria specializing in regional cuisine to savor an authentic rendition of Vitello Tonnato. Pair it with a glass of crisp Arneis or Gavi wine for a truly unforgettable dining experience.

4. Agnolotti del Plin:

Description: Agnolotti del Plin are small, hand-pinched pasta parcels filled with a savory mixture of meat, typically beef or veal, along with herbs and cheese. These delicate dumplings are then served with a rich butter and sage sauce, allowing the flavors of the filling to shine.

Exploration Tip: Join a guided food tour of Piedmont's historic towns and villages, where you can sample Agnolotti del Plin from local trattorias and family-run restaurants. Learn about the significance of this beloved dish within the region's culinary heritage while indulging in its comforting flavors.

5. Brasato al Barolo:

Description: Brasato al Barolo is a hearty dish featuring beef braised in Piedmont's famed Barolo wine, along with aromatic vegetables and herbs. The slow cooking process imbues the meat with a rich, complex flavor, while the wine-infused sauce adds depth and intensity to the dish.

Exploration Tip: Embark on a wine tour of Piedmont's Barolo-producing vineyards, where you can sample the region's renowned wines and learn about its winemaking traditions. Conclude your tour with a meal at a local trattoria, where

Brasato al Barolo is sure to be a highlight of the menu.

How Travelers Can Explore Traditional Piedmontese Cuisine:

- *Culinary Workshops and Cooking Classes:*** Participate in hands-on cooking classes led by local chefs, where you can learn to prepare traditional Piedmontese dishes using fresh, seasonal ingredients sourced from local markets.

- *Food Tours and Tastings:* Join guided food tours of Piedmont's cities, towns, and countryside, where you can explore bustling markets, artisanal shops, and family-owned eateries while sampling a diverse array of regional specialties.

- *Truffle Hunting Excursions:* Experience the thrill of truffle hunting in the rolling hills of Langhe and Roero, accompanied by expert truffle hunters and their trained dogs. Learn about the art of truffle hunting and enjoy a truffle-themed meal featuring local delicacies.

- *Wine Tours and Cellar Visits:* Discover the world-renowned wines of Piedmont, including

Barolo, Barbaresco, and Barbera, on guided wine tours of the region's vineyards and wineries. Enjoy tastings of award-winning wines paired with traditional Piedmontese dishes.

- *Dining at Local Restaurants:* Immerse yourself in Piedmont's culinary scene by dining at trattorias, osterias, and Michelin-starred restaurants that showcase the best of traditional and contemporary Piedmontese cuisine. Be sure to explore off-the-beaten-path establishments favored by locals for an authentic dining experience.

B. Recommended Restaurants and Eateries

Discover the culinary gems of Piedmont by dining at these esteemed establishments, where traditional recipes meet innovative techniques and local ingredients are celebrated with creativity and flair.

Explore the finest dining experiences Piedmont has to offer:

1. Piazza Duomo (Alba):

Description: Nestled in the heart of Alba, Piazza Duomo is a three-Michelin-starred culinary destination renowned for its exquisite cuisine and impeccable service. Helmed by Chef Enrico Crippa, the restaurant offers a contemporary interpretation of Piedmontese classics, showcasing the region's seasonal bounty with dishes that are as visually stunning as they are delicious.

Experience: Indulge in a multi-course tasting menu featuring Chef Crippa's innovative creations, which artfully blend tradition and modernity. Pair each dish with wines selected from Piazza Duomo's extensive cellar, curated to complement the flavors of the cuisine.

2. Osteria Veglio (La Morra):

Description: Perched atop a hill in the picturesque village of La Morra, Osteria Veglio offers panoramic views of the surrounding vineyards and rolling hills of the Langhe. This family-owned trattoria specializes in traditional Piedmontese fare prepared with seasonal, locally sourced ingredients, served in a warm and inviting atmosphere.

Experience: Savor the flavors of Piedmont with a leisurely lunch or dinner on Osteria Veglio's terrace, where you can sample regional specialties such as Tajarin al Tartufo, Brasato al Barolo, and carne cruda, accompanied by a selection of fine wines from the Langhe region.

3. Trattoria della Posta (Monforte d'Alba):

Description: Located in the charming hilltop town of Monforte d'Alba, Trattoria della Posta is a beloved neighborhood eatery renowned for its authentic Piedmontese cuisine and welcoming hospitality. The menu features a selection of seasonal dishes crafted from locally sourced ingredients, including handmade pastas, braised meats, and decadent desserts.

Experience: Step into Trattoria della Posta's cozy dining room and savor the flavors of Piedmont with a hearty meal accompanied by a glass of Nebbiolo or Dolcetto wine. Don't miss the opportunity to chat with the friendly staff and learn more about the region's culinary traditions.

4. Antica Corona Reale (Cervere):

Description: Housed in a historic building that once served as a royal hunting lodge, Antica Corona Reale offers a refined dining experience steeped in tradition and elegance. Led by Chef Gian Piero Vivalda, the restaurant showcases the best of Piedmontese cuisine with a focus on seasonal ingredients and classic recipes reinterpreted with a modern twist.

Experience: Treat yourself to an unforgettable dining experience at Antica Corona Reale, where you can choose from a variety of tasting menus highlighting the flavors of Piedmont. Indulge in dishes such as Vitello Tonnato, Agnolotti del Plin, and Fassona beef, expertly paired with wines from the region's prestigious vineyards.

Exploration Tips for Dining at Recommended Restaurants and Eateries:

- *Make Reservations in Advance:* Due to their popularity, reservations are highly recommended, especially during peak tourist seasons and holidays.
- *Dress Code:* Some upscale restaurants may have a dress code, so be sure to inquire when making your

reservation to ensure you comply with any requirements.

- ***Ask for Recommendations:*** Don't hesitate to ask the staff for recommendations or guidelines when selecting dishes and wines from the menu—they are experts in Piedmontese cuisine and eager to help you have an enjoyable dining experience.

- ***Explore Nearby Attractions:*** Combine your dining experience with exploration of nearby attractions, such as historic landmarks, scenic vistas, or charming villages, to make the most of your visit to Piedmont.

C. Food Markets and Specialty Shops

Immerse yourself in Piedmont's vibrant culinary scene by exploring its bustling food markets and specialty shops, where you can discover a treasure trove of local delights and artisanal products that showcase the region's rich gastronomic heritage.

Explore the vibrant food markets and specialty shops of Piedmont:

1. Mercato di Porta Palazzo (Turin):

Description: As one of Europe's largest open-air markets, Mercato di Porta Palazzo is a feast for the senses, offering an array of fresh produce, artisanal cheeses, cured meats, fragrant spices, and more. Spanning several blocks in Turin's historic center, this bustling market is a hub of activity where locals and visitors alike gather to shop, socialize, and sample the region's culinary delights.

Exploration Tip: Arrive early in the morning to experience the market at its liveliest, when vendors set up their stalls and the air is filled with the enticing aromas of freshly baked bread, ripe fruits, and roasted coffee.

2. Eataly (Turin):

Description: Eataly is a culinary emporium dedicated to celebrating the best of Italian cuisine, offering a curated selection of high-quality products sourced from local producers and artisans. Located in Turin's Lingotto district, this sprawling marketplace features multiple restaurants, cafes, and food counters, as well as a wide range of gourmet products, including pasta, olive oil, wine, cheese, and more.

Exploration Tip: Take a guided tour of Eataly to learn about the history and craftsmanship behind the products sold in the marketplace, and be sure to sample some of the delicious offerings along the way.

3. Tartuflanghe (Alba):

Description: Located in the heart of Alba, Tartuflanghe is a mecca for truffle lovers, offering an extensive selection of truffle-based products, including oils, sauces, preserves, and specialty foods. Founded by the Morra family, who have been hunting truffles in the Langhe region for generations, Tartuflanghe is committed to preserving the traditions of truffle cultivation and showcasing the unique flavors of this prized ingredient.

Exploration Tip: Join a truffle-themed workshop or tasting at Tartuflanghe to deepen your understanding of truffles and learn how to incorporate them into your cooking at home.

4. La Bottega del Barolo (Barolo):

Description: Situated in the heart of Barolo wine country, La Bottega del Barolo is a must-visit destination for wine enthusiasts seeking to explore Piedmont's world-renowned wine region. This boutique wine shop offers a curated selection of Barolo wines, as well as other regional varietals, sourced from local producers and vineyards. In addition to wine, La Bottega del Barolo also stocks a variety of wine-related accessories and gourmet products.

Exploration Tip: Attend a wine tasting or guided tour at La Bottega del Barolo to sample a selection of Piedmont's finest wines and learn about the terroir, grape varieties, and winemaking techniques that make the region unique.

Exploration Tips for Food Markets and Specialty Shops:

- *Sample Local Delicacies:* Take advantage of the opportunity to sample local specialties and artisanal products offered by vendors at the markets and shops. Be adventurous and try something new!

- **Talk to the Producers:** Engage with the vendors and producers to learn more about their products, production methods, and culinary traditions. They are often passionate about their craft and happy to share their knowledge with curious visitors.

- **Shop Responsibly:** Support local producers and artisans by purchasing their products, and consider the environmental and social impact of your purchases. Opt for sustainably sourced and ethically produced goods whenever possible.

- **Bring a Reusable Bag:** Come prepared with a reusable bag or basket to carry your purchases and minimize waste. Many markets and shops discourage the use of single-use plastic bags in favor of eco-friendly alternatives.

In Piedmont, dining is not just a meal—it's a celebration of tradition, innovation, and the art of savoring life's simple pleasures. Let your taste buds be your guide as you embark on a culinary odyssey through this gastronomic paradise.

Chapter 7: Practical Information

Before embarking on your journey to Piedmont, it's essential to familiarize yourself with some practical information to ensure a smooth and enjoyable experience. From language and communication to currency and banking, here's what you need to know:

A. Language and Communication

In Piedmont, the linguistic tapestry reflects the region's diverse cultural heritage. Italian serves as the primary language, binding the community together with its melodic cadence and expressive vocabulary. However, delve deeper into the local fabric, and you'll uncover Piedmontese, a language cherished for its historical significance and regional identity.

Italian: As you traverse the bustling streets of Turin or meander through the picturesque vineyards of Langhe, Italian will be your linguistic passport. From ordering your morning espresso at a quaint café to striking up conversations with friendly locals, mastering a few key phrases will enrich your travel experience. "Buongiorno" (good morning), "grazie" (thank you), and "prego" (you're welcome) are simple yet powerful expressions of courtesy that will endear you to the Piedmontese people. Embrace the lyrical beauty of Italian as you immerse yourself in the rich tapestry of the region's cultural tapestry.

Here are 30 Italian phrases divided into different categories that would be useful for travelers:

Greeting and Basic Courtesy:
1. Buongiorno - Good morning
2. Buonasera - Good evening
3. Ciao - Hello/Goodbye (informal)
4. Grazie - Thank you
5. Prego - You're welcome
6. Per favore - Please
7. Scusa - Excuse me (informal)
8. Mi dispiace - I'm sorry

9. Molto bene - Very well
10. Arrivederci - Goodbye

Getting Around:
11. Dov'è il bagno? - Where is the bathroom?
12. Quanto costa? - How much does it cost?
13. Posso avere il conto, per favore? - Can I have the bill, please?
14. A che ora apre/chiude? - What time does it open/close?
15. Posso prendere un taxi qui? - Can I get a taxi here?

Eating and Drinking:
16. Vorrei un caffè, per favore - I would like a coffee, please
17. Mi può consigliare un piatto tipico della regione? - Can you recommend a local dish?
18. Vorrei una birra/vino, per favore - I would like a beer/wine, please
19. Questo è delizioso! - This is delicious!
20. Non mangio carne/pesce - I don't eat meat/fish

Shopping:

21. Posso provare questo? - Can I try this on?
22. Ha questo in un'altra taglia? - Do you have this in another size?
23. Quanto costa questo? - How much is this?
24. Accettate carte di credito? - Do you accept credit cards?
25. Posso avere uno sconto? - Can I have a discount?

Emergencies:
26. Mi sento male. Mi può aiutare? - I feel sick. Can you help me?
27. Dove posso trovare un medico? - Where can I find a doctor?
28. Ho perso il mio passaporto. - I lost my passport.
29. C'è un'ambulanza? - Is there an ambulance?
30. Ho bisogno di aiuto. - I need help.

These phrases cover a range of situations that travelers may encounter during their journey in Italy and can help facilitate communication and interactions with locals.

Piedmontese: Beyond the realm of Italian lies Piedmontese, a language steeped in centuries of tradition and folklore. With its Gallo-Italic roots, Piedmontese resonates with a distinct charm that reflects the region's rural heritage. While Italian remains the dominant language in urban centers, venture into the quaint villages nestled amid the rolling hills, and you'll encounter a treasure trove of Piedmontese dialects. From the lyrical melodies of the Langhe to the rustic cadences of the Alpine valleys, each dialect tells a unique story of the land and its people. Engage with locals in their native tongue, and you'll unlock a deeper understanding of Piedmont's cultural tapestry.

Here are 30 Piedmontese phrases that can be helpful for navigating Piedmont:

Greeting and Basic Courtesy:
1. Bon di - Good morning
2. Bona sera - Good evening
3. Salve - Hello
4. Sìa or Piasènt - Please
5. Graziass - Thank you

6. Prèg or Piacé - You're welcome
7. Scusì - Excuse me
8. Dispisas - I'm sorry
9. Vèrs bèin - Very well
10. Adess or Arvèd - Goodbye

Getting Around:
11. Dòve l'é el bagno? - Where is the bathroom?
12. Quant costa? - How much does it cost?
13. L'é pensijon? - Where is the hotel?
14. A che ora s'apre/chiude? - What time does it open/close?
15. L'é l'ostaria? - Where is the restaurant?

Eating and Drinking:
16. Voréi un café, per piasènt - I would like a coffee, please
17. Che cosa mi consiglié da mangé? - What do you recommend to eat?
18. Voréi un vin, per piasènt - I would like a wine, please
19. Chè bon! - How delicious!
20. Non mangio carne/pesc - I don't eat meat/fish

Shopping:
21. Posso preuar quist? - Can I try this on?
22. L'é do stà quist antria méida? - Do you have this in another size?
23. Quanta costa quist? - How much is this?
24. Accètatee i carta? - Do you accept credit cards?
25. Mi puoi fa un spès? - Can you give me a discount?

Emergencies:
26. Mi sent mal. Mi peui ajuté? - I feel sick. Can you help me?
27. Dóve l'é 'l dotore? - Where is the doctor?
28. Ho perso il mé passapòrt. - I lost my passport.
29. Gh'é un ambulanza? - Is there an ambulance?
30. Mi serve un aiut. - I need help.

These phrases will assist travelers in navigating Piedmont while also showcasing respect for the local culture and language.

English: For travelers accustomed to the lingua franca of global communication, fear not, for English serves as a reliable bridge in Piedmont.

While proficiency may vary among the populace, you'll find that many locals, especially in tourist hubs and hospitality sectors, possess a commendable command of English. From hotel staff eager to assist you with check-in procedures to restaurant servers offering recommendations for delectable regional dishes, English opens doors to seamless communication and meaningful interactions. Embrace the opportunity to engage with locals in their native language while appreciating the convenience of English as a universal means of communication.

Practical Tips: To enhance your linguistic journey through Piedmont, consider equipping yourself with a pocket phrasebook or downloading translation apps for on-the-go assistance. Practice basic Italian phrases such as "Dov'è il bagno?" (Where is the bathroom?) and "Quanto costa?" (How much does it cost?) to navigate everyday situations with ease. Embrace the cultural nuances of language, from the animated hand gestures of Italian conversation to the warm hospitality embodied in Piedmontese dialects. By embracing the diverse linguistic landscape of Piedmont, you'll embark on a journey of cultural discovery that transcends mere words.

By acquainting yourself with these practical details, you'll be well-prepared to immerse yourself in the enchanting landscapes, rich culture, and culinary delights that await you in Piedmont. Travel with an open mind, a spirit of adventure, and a willingness to embrace the beauty of this captivating region. Buon viaggio!

B. Currency and Money Matters

When planning a trip to Piedmont, Italy, understanding the currency and managing your money effectively are essential aspects of ensuring a smooth and enjoyable experience. From knowing the local currency to handling transactions and accessing funds, here's everything you need to know about currency and money matters in Piedmont.

The Euro (EUR)

Italy, including the Piedmont region, utilizes the Euro (EUR) as its official currency. The Euro is denoted by the symbol "€" and is divided into 100 cents. Banknotes come in various denominations, including €5, €10, €20, €50, €100, €200, and €500, while coins are available in 1, 2, 5, 10, 20, and 50 cents, as well as €1 and €2 denominations.

Currency Exchange

Before embarking on your journey to Piedmont, it's advisable to exchange your currency for Euros. Currency exchange services are readily available at airports, banks, currency exchange offices, and some hotels. While airport exchanges may be convenient, they often offer less favorable exchange rates compared to other options. Banks and dedicated currency exchange offices typically provide better rates, so consider exchanging your currency there for optimal value.

ATMs and Cash Withdrawals

ATMs (Automated Teller Machines) are prevalent throughout Piedmont, particularly in urban areas such as Turin, Alba, and Asti, as well as in popular tourist destinations. They offer a convenient way to access Euros directly from your bank account using your debit or credit card. Most ATMs in Italy support international cards, including those issued by major networks such as Visa, Mastercard, and Maestro.

When withdrawing cash from ATMs, be mindful of potential fees charged by your bank for international transactions and currency conversion. Additionally, ensure you inform your bank of your travel plans beforehand to prevent any issues with accessing funds abroad.

Credit and Debit Cards

Credit and debit cards are widely accepted in Piedmont, particularly in larger establishments such as hotels, restaurants, shops, and tourist attractions. Visa and Mastercard are the most commonly accepted card networks, followed by

American Express and Discover, although acceptance may vary depending on the establishment.

When using your card for transactions, you may be prompted to choose between paying in Euros or your home currency (Dynamic Currency Conversion). Opting to pay in Euros typically offers better exchange rates, so select this option whenever possible to avoid additional fees associated with currency conversion.

Tips for Managing Money

To ensure a hassle-free experience managing your money in Piedmont, consider the following tips:

1. Carry Sufficient Cash: While credit and debit cards are widely accepted, it's always wise to carry some cash for smaller purchases, street vendors, and establishments that may not accept cards.

2. Notify Your Bank: Inform your bank of your travel plans, including the dates and destinations,

to prevent any potential issues with card usage abroad.

3. Keep Emergency Funds: Stash away some emergency cash in a secure location, such as a money belt or hidden pocket, for unexpected situations or emergencies.

4. Monitor Exchange Rates: Stay informed about current exchange rates to maximize the value of your currency exchanges and transactions.

By familiarizing yourself with the currency and money matters in Piedmont and adopting prudent financial practices, you can enjoy a worry-free and fulfilling travel experience in this captivating region of Italy.

C. Packing Lists for Piedmont

Preparing for a trip to Piedmont involves thoughtful consideration of the region's diverse activities, climates, and cultural experiences. Whether you're exploring the bustling streets of

Turin, hiking through the majestic Alps, or savoring the renowned wines of the Langhe region, packing strategically ensures you're equipped for every adventure. Here's a comprehensive packing list tailored to the varied experiences awaiting you in Piedmont:

Clothing:

1. Layered Clothing: Piedmont's weather can vary widely, so pack lightweight clothing for warm days and layers for cooler evenings or higher elevations.
2. Comfortable Walking Shoes: Whether strolling through city streets or trekking along hiking trails, supportive and comfortable footwear is essential.
3. Rain Jacket or Umbrella: Be prepared for occasional showers by packing a waterproof jacket or compact umbrella.
4. Warm Outerwear: If traveling during the colder months or planning mountain excursions, bring a warm jacket, hat, gloves, and scarf.

5. Swimwear: If visiting during the summer, don't forget your swimsuit for relaxing by the pool or enjoying the beaches of nearby lakes.

Travel Essentials:

1. Reusable Water Bottle: Stay hydrated throughout your adventures by carrying a refillable water bottle.
2. Sun Protection: Pack sunscreen, sunglasses, and a wide-brimmed hat to shield yourself from the sun's rays.
3. Daypack or Tote Bag: A lightweight and versatile bag is perfect for carrying essentials during day trips and excursions.
4. Travel Adapter: Ensure your electronics stay charged by bringing a universal adapter compatible with Italian electrical outlets (Type C and Type F).
5. Portable Power Bank: Keep your devices charged on the go with a portable power bank, especially useful for extended outings or photography enthusiasts.

Toiletries and Personal Care:

1. Basic Toiletries: Bring travel-sized toiletries, including shampoo, conditioner, soap, toothpaste, and a toothbrush.

2. First Aid Kit: Pack essential medications, bandages, antiseptic wipes, and any other necessary medical supplies.

3. Insect Repellent: Protect yourself from mosquitoes and other insects, particularly if spending time outdoors or in rural areas.

4. Hand Sanitizer: Maintain good hygiene practices by carrying hand sanitizer for convenient disinfection when soap and water are unavailable.

Miscellaneous Items:

1. Guidebooks and Maps: Enhance your exploration of Piedmont with guidebooks, maps, or digital travel apps to discover hidden gems and navigate unfamiliar areas.

2. Travel Documents: Ensure you have all necessary travel documents, including your passport, visa (if required), travel insurance information, and any reservations or confirmations.

3. **Reusable Shopping Bag:** Reduce waste and be prepared for impromptu purchases by carrying a foldable shopping bag.

Optional Extras:

1. Camera and Accessories: Capture memorable moments of your Piedmont adventure with a camera and accessories, such as extra batteries and memory cards.

2. Language Phrasebook: Brush up on essential Italian phrases or use a translation app to facilitate communication with locals.

By packing thoughtfully and considering the specific activities and environments you'll encounter in Piedmont, you can optimize your travel experience and create lasting memories in this enchanting region of Italy.

D. Safety Tips and Emergency Contacts

While Piedmont is generally a safe destination for travelers, it's essential to prioritize your well-being and take precautions to ensure a smooth and enjoyable trip. By staying informed, exercising common sense, and being prepared for emergencies, you can mitigate risks and focus on making the most of your time in this captivating region. Here are some safety tips and emergency contacts to keep in mind:

1. Stay Informed:

   - Research Your Destination: Familiarize yourself with the local customs, laws, and potential safety concerns of Piedmont before your trip.
   - Stay Updated: Monitor local news and weather updates for any developments that may affect your travel plans or safety.

2. Exercise Caution:

- Be Vigilant in Crowded Areas: Stay alert and aware of your surroundings, particularly in crowded tourist attractions, markets, and public transportation hubs, where pickpocketing and petty theft may occur.

- Avoid Risky Situations: Use caution when exploring unfamiliar areas, especially at night, and avoid walking alone in poorly lit or isolated areas.

3. Secure Your Belongings:

- Keep Valuables Secure: Carry only essential items with you and keep valuables such as passports, cash, and electronics securely stored in a hotel safe or hidden pouch.

- Use Secure Bags: Opt for crossbody bags or backpacks with anti-theft features to deter theft.

4. Stay Healthy:

- Stay Hydrated and Sun Protected: Drink plenty of water, especially during hot weather, and protect yourself from the sun's harmful rays with sunscreen, hats, and sunglasses.

- Practice Food Safety: Enjoy Piedmont's culinary delights while being mindful of food hygiene practices to prevent foodborne illnesses.

5. *Emergency Contacts:*

- Emergency Services: In case of emergency, dial 112 for police, medical assistance, or firefighting services.

- Embassy or Consulate: Locate the nearest embassy or consulate of your home country in Italy for assistance with passport issues, emergencies, or other consular services.

6. *Travel Insurance:*

- Obtain Travel Insurance: Consider purchasing travel insurance that provides coverage for medical emergencies, trip cancellations, and other unforeseen events to protect yourself and your investment in case of emergencies.

7. *Natural Hazards:*

- Be Aware of Natural Hazards: If engaging in outdoor activities such as hiking or skiing, familiarize yourself with potential risks such as avalanches, sudden weather changes, and wildlife encounters, and take appropriate precautions.

8. Follow Local Laws and Customs:

- Respect Local Customs: Familiarize yourself with local customs and cultural norms, including dress codes and etiquette, to show respect for the local culture and avoid unintentional offenses.

By following these safety tips and being prepared for emergencies, you can enjoy a worry-free and rewarding travel experience in Piedmont, Italy. Remember to stay vigilant, trust your instincts, and prioritize your safety and well-being throughout your journey.

In conclusion, by following these practical tips, you can make the most of your trip to Piedmont while staying safe and prepared for any situation.

Chapter 8: Piedmont for Families

Piedmont, with its rich cultural heritage, stunning landscapes, and delicious cuisine, offers a plethora of opportunities for families to create unforgettable memories together. From exploring historic sites to indulging in mouthwatering local delicacies, there's something for everyone in this charming region of Italy.

A. Family-friendly Attractions and Activities

Piedmont offers an array of family-friendly attractions and activities that cater to both kids and adults alike. From historical landmarks to culinary adventures, there's no shortage of entertainment for families exploring this charming region of Italy.

Exploring Historical Landmarks

One of the highlights of visiting Piedmont with your family is the opportunity to explore its rich historical heritage. The Egyptian Museum in Turin, for example, is a must-visit attraction that offers a fascinating glimpse into ancient civilizations. Kids will be captivated by the museum's collection of mummies, sarcophagi, and hieroglyphics, while parents can appreciate the museum's role in preserving and showcasing Egypt's cultural legacy.

Another iconic landmark worth visiting is the Sacra di San Michele, a medieval abbey located atop Mount Pirchiriano. Accessible via a scenic hike or cable car ride, the Sacra di San Michele offers breathtaking views of the surrounding landscape and provides families with an opportunity to learn about the abbey's fascinating history and architecture.

Outdoor Adventures

For families who love the great outdoors, Piedmont offers a wealth of opportunities for adventure and exploration. The Gran Paradiso National Park, Italy's oldest national park, is a paradise for nature lovers, with its rugged mountains, pristine lakes, and diverse wildlife. Families can embark on guided hikes, spot ibex and chamois, and marvel at the park's stunning alpine scenery.

Closer to Turin, the Parco del Valentino provides families with a tranquil retreat in the heart of the city. With its manicured gardens, tree-lined paths, and playgrounds, the park offers ample space for children to run and play while parents relax and enjoy a leisurely stroll along the river.

Culinary Delights

No trip to Piedmont would be complete without indulging in its world-renowned cuisine. From creamy risottos to decadent chocolates, the region offers a feast for the senses that is sure to please even the pickiest eaters.

Families can embark on a chocolate tour in Turin, where they can visit artisanal chocolate shops, learn about the chocolate-making process, and sample a variety of sweet treats. For a more hands-on experience, families can visit a local farm to learn about cheese-making and even try their hand at crafting their own cheese.

Scenic Tours

To truly appreciate the beauty of Piedmont, families can embark on scenic tours that showcase the region's stunning landscapes and picturesque villages. A boat tour along Lake Maggiore, for example, offers families the opportunity to cruise past charming waterfront towns, lush vineyards, and historic castles while enjoying panoramic views of the surrounding mountains.

Similarly, a ride on the historic Turin Tram provides families with a unique way to explore the city's landmarks and attractions. As the tram winds its way through Turin's bustling streets, families can hop on and off at various stops to visit museums, piazzas, and cultural sites, making for a memorable and educational experience for all.

B. Parks and Playgrounds

Piedmont boasts an abundance of parks and playgrounds where families can unwind, play, and connect with nature. Whether you're seeking a peaceful retreat or an action-packed day of fun, the region offers a variety of outdoor spaces that cater to families of all ages and interests.

Parco del Valentino

Located in the heart of Turin, Parco del Valentino is a beloved destination for families seeking relaxation and recreation. Stretching along the banks of the Po River, this expansive park features lush greenery, winding pathways, and scenic views that provide the perfect backdrop for picnics, leisurely strolls, and outdoor activities.

Children will delight in the park's playgrounds, which are equipped with swings, slides, and climbing structures designed to spark their imagination and encourage active play. Meanwhile, parents can unwind on park benches or enjoy a leisurely boat ride along the river, taking in the sights and sounds of nature.

Gran Paradiso National Park

For families seeking adventure amid breathtaking natural scenery, Gran Paradiso National Park offers an unparalleled outdoor experience. Situated in the heart of the Western Alps, this vast wilderness sanctuary is home to towering peaks, pristine alpine lakes, and diverse ecosystems teeming with wildlife.

Families can explore the park's network of hiking trails, ranging from gentle paths suitable for young children to challenging routes for experienced adventurers. Along the way, they may encounter ibex, chamois, and other native species, providing opportunities for wildlife viewing and nature photography.

Parco della Mandria

Nestled in the countryside just outside of Turin, Parco della Mandria offers families a tranquil escape from the hustle and bustle of city life. Once a royal hunting estate, this sprawling park is now a protected natural reserve, boasting forests, meadows, and historical landmarks that reflect its rich heritage.

Families can spend the day exploring the park's scenic trails on foot or by bike, discovering hidden ponds, ancient ruins, and charming farmhouses along the way. With designated picnic areas and barbecue spots, Parco della Mandria is also an ideal setting for alfresco dining and enjoying quality time together amidst nature's beauty.

Monte dei Cappuccini

For panoramic views of Turin and the surrounding countryside, families can ascend Monte dei Cappuccini, a scenic hilltop located just across the river from the city center. A short hike or funicular ride leads to the summit, where visitors are rewarded with breathtaking vistas and the opportunity to explore the hilltop's historic monastery and gardens.

Children can roam freely in the open spaces, while parents soak in the beauty of the landscape and capture memorable photos of their family against the backdrop of Turin's iconic skyline. Whether picnicking in the park, hiking in the mountains, or enjoying a leisurely stroll, Piedmont's parks and playgrounds offer endless opportunities for families to connect with each other and with the natural world.

C. Kid-friendly Restaurants and Accommodations

Piedmont welcomes families with a wide selection of kid-friendly restaurants and accommodations, ensuring that parents and children alike can enjoy a comfortable and memorable experience during their visit to the region. From charming trattorias serving up traditional Piedmontese fare to family-friendly hotels equipped with amenities catering to children's needs, there are plenty of options to choose from.

Trattorias and Pizzerias

In Piedmont's charming towns and cities, trattorias and pizzerias abound, offering hearty and delicious meals that are sure to please even the pickiest eaters. These family-friendly eateries often feature kid-friendly menus with familiar favorites like pizza, pasta, and gelato, as well as regional specialties such as agnolotti and tajarin.

Many trattorias also provide high chairs, children's menus, and coloring activities to keep little ones entertained while parents enjoy a leisurely meal. With their warm hospitality and relaxed atmosphere, these establishments offer the perfect setting for families to gather and savor the flavors of Piedmont together.

Agriturismos

For families seeking a taste of rural life, agriturismos offer a unique and immersive experience that combines farm stays with authentic Piedmontese hospitality. These family-run accommodations are typically located on working farms or vineyards, allowing guests to participate in agricultural activities such as harvesting grapes, feeding animals, and making cheese.

Children will delight in the opportunity to interact with farm animals, explore the countryside, and learn about traditional farming practices firsthand. Meanwhile, parents can relax and unwind amidst the picturesque surroundings, savoring farm-fresh meals made with locally sourced ingredients and enjoying wine tastings featuring the region's renowned vintages.

Family-Friendly Hotels

In Piedmont's cities and tourist destinations, families will find a variety of hotels and guesthouses that cater to their needs with amenities and services designed specifically for children. Many hotels offer family suites or interconnected rooms, providing ample space for families to spread out and relax.

Kids clubs, playgrounds, and swimming pools are common features at family-friendly hotels, offering children plenty of opportunities for fun and entertainment while parents enjoy some well-deserved downtime. Babysitting services, cribs, and child-friendly dining options are also available to ensure that families have everything they need for a comfortable and stress-free stay.

Self-Catering Accommodations

For families who prefer the flexibility of self-catering, Piedmont offers a variety of vacation rentals and holiday apartments equipped with kitchenettes or full kitchens. These accommodations provide families with the freedom to prepare meals according to their preferences and dietary requirements, making it easy to accommodate picky eaters or special dietary needs.

With spacious living areas, multiple bedrooms, and convenient amenities like washing machines and Wi-Fi, self-catering accommodations offer families the comforts of home combined with the excitement of travel. Whether staying in a rustic farmhouse in the countryside or a modern apartment in the city, families will find plenty of options to suit their needs and budget in Piedmont.

With its wealth of attractions, beautiful landscapes, and welcoming atmosphere, Piedmont is the perfect destination for families looking to create lasting memories together. Whether exploring historic sites, enjoying outdoor adventures, or savoring delicious cuisine, there's no shortage of things to see and do in this enchanting region of Italy.

Chapter 9: Itinerary Planning

Planning the perfect itinerary is essential for making the most out of your journey through Piedmont. Whether you have a week, 10 days, or two weeks to explore this enchanting region, careful planning ensures you don't miss out on its diverse cultural, culinary, and natural attractions.

A. Sample Itineraries for 1 Week, 10 Days, and 2 Weeks

When planning your trip to Piedmont, it's essential to consider how much time you have available to explore this diverse region. Whether you're a wine enthusiast, a history buff, or a nature lover, Piedmont offers something for everyone. Here are sample itineraries tailored to different durations of stay:

1. One Week Itinerary

If you have only one week to spare, focus your itinerary on experiencing the highlights of Piedmont, from its vibrant cities to its picturesque countryside.

Day 1-2: Turin
Begin your journey in the capital city of Turin, where history and modernity blend seamlessly. Spend your first day exploring the historic city center, strolling through Piazza Castello, and marveling at the grandeur of the Royal Palace. Don't miss the opportunity to visit the Turin Cathedral and view the famous Shroud of Turin. On your second day, delve into Turin's rich cultural heritage with a visit to the Egyptian Museum, home to an impressive collection of ancient artifacts. Indulge in a chocolate tasting tour to sample some of the city's finest creations.

Day 3-4: Langhe Region
Venture into the picturesque Langhe region, renowned for its rolling hills, vineyards, and gourmet cuisine. Spend a day exploring the charming towns of Barolo and Barbaresco, known

for their world-class wines. Take a leisurely drive through the countryside, stopping at local wineries to taste Barolo, Nebbiolo, and Barbera wines. On your fourth day, immerse yourself in the world of truffles with a truffle hunting experience in Alba, followed by a decadent truffle-infused meal at a traditional trattoria.

Day 5-7: Lake Maggiore

Conclude your week with a relaxing retreat to Lake Maggiore, one of Italy's most enchanting lakes. Take a boat tour to the Borromean Islands, where you can explore the opulent gardens of Isola Bella and visit the picturesque village of Isola dei Pescatori. Spend your remaining days soaking in the serene beauty of Lake Maggiore, whether lounging on its shores, indulging in water sports, or taking leisurely boat rides to nearby towns like Stresa and Pallanza.

B. Ten Days Itinerary

For those with a bit more time to spare, a ten-day itinerary allows for a deeper exploration of

Piedmont's diverse landscapes and cultural treasures.

Day 8-10: Lake Orta and Valsesia

Extend your journey with a visit to the tranquil Lake Orta, often overlooked by tourists but beloved by those in the know. Explore the charming village of Orta San Giulio, with its cobbled streets and medieval buildings. Take a boat ride to Isola San Giulio and discover its historic basilica and monastery. Continue your adventure with a drive to the rugged Valsesia region, where you can hike through the scenic Sesia Valley and visit the Sacro Monte di Varallo, a UNESCO World Heritage site showcasing religious art and architecture.

Two Weeks Itinerary

For the ultimate Piedmont experience, immerse yourself in the region's rich history, culture, and natural beauty with a two-week itinerary.

Day 11-14: Piedmont Countryside and Alps

Spend your final days exploring the picturesque countryside of Piedmont and venturing into the majestic Alps. Drive through the scenic landscapes of the Monferrato and Roero regions, dotted with medieval castles, vineyards, and hilltop villages. Visit the charming town of Asti, renowned for its sparkling wines, and indulge in a wine tasting tour of the surrounding vineyards. Conclude your journey with a scenic drive through the Alps, stopping at picturesque mountain villages like Limone Piemonte and Sestriere, where you can enjoy hiking, skiing, or simply soaking in the breathtaking views.

With these carefully crafted itineraries, you can make the most of your time in Piedmont and create memories that will last a lifetime. Whether you're exploring historic cities, savoring gourmet cuisine, or admiring stunning natural landscapes, Piedmont is sure to captivate your heart and soul.

B. Day-by-Day Breakdown of Activities and Sightseeing

To make the most of your time in Piedmont, it's essential to plan your day-by-day activities and sightseeing adventures carefully. Here's a detailed breakdown of what to expect each day during your journey through this captivating region:

Day 1: Arrival in Turin

Upon your arrival in Turin, take some time to settle into your accommodation and familiarize yourself with the city. Depending on your arrival time, you may want to begin exploring the city center, taking in iconic landmarks such as Piazza Castello and the Mole Antonelliana. Enjoy a leisurely dinner at a local trattoria to kick off your Piedmontese culinary experience.

Day 2: Turin Sightseeing

Dedicate your second day to exploring the vibrant city of Turin in more depth. Start your morning with a visit to the Royal Palace of Turin, home to the Savoy dynasty for centuries. Explore its opulent rooms and expansive gardens before heading to the nearby Turin Cathedral to marvel at its stunning Renaissance architecture and the Shroud of Turin. Spend the afternoon wandering through the bustling streets of the city center, browsing shops, and indulging in gelato from one of Turin's famed gelaterias.

Day 3: Transfer to Langhe Region

On your third day, bid farewell to Turin and venture into the enchanting Langhe region. Take a scenic drive through rolling hills and vineyards to reach your destination. Once you arrive, spend the afternoon exploring the charming town of Barolo, known for its world-class wines. Visit local wineries to taste Barolo and other regional varietals before enjoying a traditional Piedmontese dinner paired with the finest local wines.

Day 4: Wine Tasting and Truffle Hunting

Continue your exploration of the Langhe region with a day dedicated to wine tasting and truffle hunting. Visit the town of Barbaresco, famous for its eponymous wine, and sample its distinctive flavors at family-run wineries. In the afternoon, embark on a truffle hunting experience in the nearby town of Alba, accompanied by expert truffle hunters and their trusty dogs. Learn about the art of truffle hunting and enjoy a delicious truffle-infused meal at a local trattoria.

Day 5: Lake Maggiore

Say goodbye to the Langhe region and journey to the serene shores of Lake Maggiore. Take a boat tour to the Borromean Islands, where you can explore the elaborate gardens of Isola Bella and visit the charming village of Isola dei Pescatori. Spend the rest of the day relaxing by the lake, perhaps indulging in water sports or simply soaking in the breathtaking views.

Day 6: Exploring Stresa and Pallanza

Explore the picturesque lakeside towns of Stresa and Pallanza on your sixth day in Piedmont. Stroll along the waterfront promenades, admire the elegant Belle Époque architecture, and visit historic landmarks such as Villa Pallavicino and the Church of San Vittore. In the afternoon, take a leisurely boat ride on Lake Maggiore, stopping at scenic viewpoints and hidden coves along the way.

Day 7: Leisure Day at Lake Maggiore

Savor your final day in Piedmont with a leisurely day at Lake Maggiore. Spend the morning exploring the quaint streets of nearby towns, browsing local markets, and sampling regional delicacies. In the afternoon, relax on the shores of the lake, perhaps indulging in a spa treatment or taking a scenic bike ride along the lakeside trails. As the sun sets, enjoy a farewell dinner overlooking the tranquil waters of Lake Maggiore, reflecting on the unforgettable experiences of your Piedmont adventure.

C. Tips for Maximizing Time and Experiences

Making the most out of your journey through Piedmont requires careful planning and consideration of various factors. Here are some invaluable tips to help you maximize your time and experiences in this captivating region:

1. Plan Ahead

Research and plan your itinerary well in advance to ensure you make the most of your time in Piedmont. Identify the attractions and activities that interest you the most and prioritize them in your schedule. Book accommodations, transportation, and tours ahead of time to avoid last-minute hassles and ensure availability during peak seasons.

2. Be Flexible

While planning is essential, it's also important to remain flexible and open to spontaneous experiences. Allow for some free time in your itinerary to explore unexpected discoveries or take advantage of local recommendations from residents or fellow travelers. Embrace the serendipity of travel and be willing to adjust your plans as needed to make the most of your time in Piedmont.

3. Use Local Transport

Take advantage of Piedmont's efficient public transportation system, including trains, buses, and boats, to navigate between cities and regions. Not only will this save you time and money, but it will also allow you to experience the local culture and scenery along the way. Consider renting a car for exploring rural areas and remote villages at your own pace.

4. Prioritize Must-See Attractions

With limited time available, prioritize the must-see attractions and experiences that align with your interests. Whether it's visiting historic landmarks, indulging in gourmet cuisine, or exploring natural wonders, focus on the activities that resonate with you the most. Be realistic about what you can accomplish in a day and avoid overloading your itinerary with too many activities.

5. *Take Breaks*

Traveling can be exhausting, so be sure to schedule downtime to rest and recharge during your trip. Allow yourself time to relax and unwind, whether it's lounging by the pool, enjoying a leisurely meal at a local restaurant, or simply taking a leisurely stroll through a scenic park. Taking breaks will help prevent burnout and ensure you have the energy to fully enjoy your Piedmont experience.

6. *Embrace Local Culture*

Immerse yourself in the rich cultural heritage of Piedmont by participating in local traditions, festivals, and events. Attend a wine tasting or cooking class to learn about traditional Piedmontese cuisine, or explore the region's vibrant arts and music scene. Engage with locals and learn about their way of life, gaining insights into the authentic beauty of Piedmont beyond its tourist attractions.

By following these tips, you can make the most of your time in Piedmont and create unforgettable memories that will last a lifetime. Whether you're exploring historic cities, savoring gourmet cuisine, or admiring stunning natural landscapes, Piedmont offers endless opportunities for discovery and adventure.

Chapter 10: Relaxation and Wellness Retreats

In a region as diverse and captivating as Piedmont, where the pace of life can sometimes be brisk, finding moments of relaxation and rejuvenation is essential. Fortunately, Piedmont offers a plethora of options for those seeking to unwind and replenish their spirits. From luxurious spa resorts nestled in the tranquil countryside to ancient thermal baths renowned for their healing properties, Piedmont provides a haven for those in search of wellness and serenity.

A. Thermal Baths and Hot Springs

Piedmont's thermal baths and hot springs have long been revered for their therapeutic properties and rejuvenating effects, drawing visitors from far and wide to experience the healing power of these natural wonders. Nestled amidst the region's breathtaking landscapes, these ancient thermal baths offer a sanctuary for those seeking relief from aches, pains, and ailments, as well as a respite from the stresses of modern life.

One of Piedmont's most iconic thermal destinations is the town of Acqui Terme, renowned for its historic Roman baths dating back to antiquity. Built by the Romans in the 2nd century BC, these ancient thermal waters are believed to possess a myriad of health benefits, including relief from arthritis, rheumatism, and respiratory ailments. Visitors to Acqui Terme can immerse themselves in the rejuvenating waters of the hot springs, which flow from deep underground at temperatures ranging from warm to scalding hot, depending on the source.

In addition to its historic Roman baths, Piedmont is also home to a wealth of natural hot springs scattered throughout the region's picturesque countryside. From the rugged mountains of the Val di Susa to the tranquil valleys of the Langhe and Roero, these hidden gems offer visitors the opportunity to unwind in secluded settings surrounded by pristine nature. Whether soaking in a rustic outdoor pool nestled amidst alpine meadows or luxuriating in a modern spa facility with panoramic views of the rolling hills, guests can experience the therapeutic benefits of Piedmont's hot springs in a variety of idyllic settings.

One such hidden gem is the thermal spa town of Lurisia, nestled amidst the lush forests of the Maritime Alps. Here, visitors can immerse themselves in the healing waters of the local hot springs, which are rich in minerals and renowned for their soothing effects on the skin and muscles. Surrounded by verdant woodlands and majestic mountains, Lurisia offers a tranquil retreat for those seeking relaxation, rejuvenation, and renewal amidst nature's splendor.

In addition to its therapeutic waters, Piedmont's thermal baths also offer a range of wellness treatments and spa services aimed at enhancing the overall spa experience. From indulgent massages and body wraps to detoxifying saunas and steam rooms, guests can pamper themselves with a variety of luxurious treatments designed to promote relaxation, detoxification, and well-being. With a commitment to holistic wellness and natural beauty, Piedmont's thermal baths and hot springs provide a sanctuary for travelers seeking to rejuvenate their bodies, minds, and spirits amidst the region's timeless charm and tranquility.

B. Yoga and Meditation Retreats

In the serene landscapes of Piedmont, amidst the rolling hills and tranquil valleys, lies a haven for those seeking inner peace and spiritual renewal. Piedmont's yoga and meditation retreats offer a sanctuary for guests to disconnect from the stresses of daily life and reconnect with themselves in a peaceful and nurturing environment.

Set amidst picturesque vineyards, olive groves, and lush countryside, Piedmont's yoga and meditation retreats provide the perfect backdrop for self-reflection and personal growth. Surrounded by nature's beauty, guests can embark on a journey of self-discovery as they explore the ancient practices of yoga and meditation under the guidance of experienced instructors and spiritual teachers.

Whether practicing gentle Hatha yoga poses amidst the serenity of a sun-dappled vineyard or finding inner stillness through guided meditation sessions in a tranquil garden, guests can experience a profound sense of relaxation and rejuvenation as they connect with the present moment and cultivate mindfulness.

Piedmont's yoga and meditation retreats offer a variety of programs and experiences tailored to suit the needs and preferences of guests of all levels and backgrounds. From immersive weekend retreats focused on relaxation and stress relief to transformative week-long programs aimed at deepening one's spiritual practice, there is something for everyone seeking solace and serenity amidst Piedmont's breathtaking landscapes.

In addition to daily yoga and meditation sessions, guests at Piedmont's retreats can indulge in a variety of holistic therapies and wellness activities designed to promote overall well-being. From rejuvenating spa treatments and healing massages to organic farm-to-table cuisine and guided nature walks, guests can nourish their bodies, minds, and spirits with nourishing experiences that honor the connection between inner and outer harmony.

Piedmont's yoga and meditation retreats also offer the opportunity to immerse oneself in the region's rich cultural heritage and culinary traditions. From wine tastings and cooking classes to visits to local markets and historical landmarks, guests can explore the essence of Piedmont and discover the timeless beauty and charm that make this region truly special.

Overall, Piedmont's yoga and meditation retreats offer a sanctuary for those seeking solace, serenity, and spiritual renewal amidst the region's breathtaking landscapes and timeless beauty. With a commitment to holistic wellness and personal growth, these retreats provide the perfect environment for guests to reconnect with themselves, cultivate mindfulness, and find inner peace in the heart of Piedmont's tranquil countryside.

In conclusion, Piedmont's relaxation and wellness retreats offer a harmonious blend of indulgence, rejuvenation, and cultural immersion. Whether seeking serenity amidst breathtaking landscapes or delving into the region's rich traditions, visitors are sure to find moments of bliss and tranquility in this captivating corner of Italy.

CONCLUSION

As we come to the end of our journey through the pages of the Piedmont Travel Guide 2024, I want to take a moment to express my sincere gratitude to you for choosing this book as your companion on your exploration of Piedmont. Your decision to embark on this adventure with us speaks volumes about your adventurous spirit and your passion for discovery, and for that, we are truly grateful.

Throughout the pages of this guide, we have endeavored to provide you with a comprehensive glimpse into the beauty, culture, and allure of Piedmont, a region that holds a special place in the hearts of all who have had the privilege to experience its charms. From the majestic peaks of the Alps to the rolling hills of the Langhe and Roero, from the vibrant cities of Turin and Asti to the quaint villages nestled amidst vineyards and olive groves, Piedmont offers a tapestry of experiences waiting to be explored.

In these pages, we have delved into the rich history and cultural heritage of Piedmont, uncovering its ancient traditions, culinary delights, and artistic treasures. We have guided you through its scenic landscapes and picturesque villages, inviting you to immerse yourself in the timeless beauty and charm that make this region truly unique.

We have also shared with you practical tips and recommendations to help you make the most of your time in Piedmont, from where to stay and what to eat to how to navigate its winding roads and bustling markets. Whether you are a seasoned traveler or a first-time visitor, we hope that the information provided in this guide has enhanced your experience and enriched your understanding of this captivating corner of Italy.

As you continue your journey through Piedmont, I encourage you to embrace every moment with an open heart and an adventurous spirit. Explore its hidden gems, savor its flavors, and immerse yourself in its vibrant culture. Let the beauty of

Piedmont inspire you, and may each new discovery fill your heart with joy and wonder.

In closing, I want to express my deepest gratitude to you for allowing us to be a part of your journey through Piedmont. It has been an honor and a privilege to accompany you on this adventure, and I hope that the memories you create here will stay with you long after your journey has ended.

May your travels be filled with joy, laughter, and unforgettable experiences, and may Piedmont forever hold a special place in your heart.

Safe travels!

Warmest regards,

[David C. Anaya]

Printed in Great Britain
by Amazon